FIFTH EDITION

UNDERSTANDING SOCIAL ISSUES

CRITICAL THINKING AND ANALYSIS

Gai Berlage
Iona College

William Egelman
Iona College

Allyn and Bacon
Boston • London • Toronto • Sydney • Tokyo • Singapore

To our children, Aaron and Jeremy Egelman
and Jan and Cari Berlage

Editor in Chief: Karen Hanson
Editorial Assistant: Jennifer Muroff
Marketing Manager: Suzie Spivey
Editorial-Production Service: Chestnut Hill Enterprises, Inc.
Manufacturing Buyer: Megan Cochran
Cover Administrator: Jennifer Hart

Copyright © 1999, 1996, 1993, 1990, 1987 by Allyn & Bacon
A Viacom Company
160 Gould Street
Needham Heights, MA 02194

Internet: www.abacon.com
America Online: keyword: College Online

Between the time Website information is gathered and published, some sites may have closed. Also, the transcription of URLs can result in typographical errors. The publisher would appreciate notification where these occur so that they may be corrected in subsequent editions. Thank you.

Library of Congress Cataloging-in-Publication Data

Berlage, Gai.
    Understanding social issues : critical thinking and analysis / Gai
Berlage, William Egelman. — 5th ed.
      p. cm.
    Includes bibliographical references.
    ISBN 0-205-27613-X (pbk.)
    1. United States—Social conditions—1980—Problems, exercises,
etc. 2. Social problems—Problems, exercises, etc. I. Egelman,
William. II. Title.
HN59.2.B46 1998
306'.0973—dc21   98-14649
                                  CIP

Printed in the United States of America

10 9 8 7 6 5 4 3 2 1   03 02 01 00 99 98

CONTENTS

Preface   v

Introduction   vii

MODULE   1 Where Will You Be Living in Five Years?   1

2 Who's Bringing Up the Children?   11

3 Are Teenage Out-of-Wedlock Births a Social Problem?   23

4 Are Gender Roles Still Sex-Typed?   33

5 Is America a Drug Culture?   45

6 Two-Fisted Jane: Myth or Reality?   55

7 Does It Pay to Go to College?   69

8 Are We Still a Nation of Immigrants?   79

9 Does Equality Exist in America?   87

10 Can You Afford to Get Sick?   99

11 AIDS: The Modern Plague?   113

12 Are We Destroying Our Environment?   121

13 Are All Marriages Doomed to Fail?   129

14 Why Worry about the Rest of the World?   137

PREFACE

The fifth edition of *Understanding Social Issues,* like earlier editions, is designed to give you, the student, an opportunity to examine current social issues. Fourteen social issues are presented, ranging from personal, such as "Where Will You Be Living in Five Years?" to national, such as "Are We Destroying Our Environment?" to international, such as "Why Worry about the Rest of the World?" Crime, drugs, AIDS, health care, childcare are some of the issues you will analyze.

This textbook is different from your other textbooks in that you are given the opportunity to be the researcher and play the role of sociologist. Each module poses a question of social importance that you are asked to analyze and to answer. You will analyze the question by using current national and international statistics, which are contained in each module. In this way, you will learn how to use available statistical data, such as the U.S. Bureau of the Census and the Federal Bureau of Investigation *Uniform Crime Reports,* to analyze social issues. You will learn how to distinguish between objective facts and subjective opinion. You will learn the difference between scientific research and hearsay. We hope that you will become so enthusiastic about the joys of doing social research that you will begin to research other issues on your own. You may begin to see college, community, national, and international issues in a new light. You may even find yourself becoming an active participant in trying to determine social policy. We would appreciate hearing from you, instructor or student, as to your comments and suggestions for topics for future editions. We are grateful to our students and colleagues who commented on the fourth edition of this book.

We especially want to thank the many people who were important in the production of this book. Allyn and Bacon provided us with excellent editorial assistance. Karen Hanson, our editor, offered us her wisdom and expertise.

G.B.
W.E.

INTRODUCTION

There are many reasons why you may have registered for a sociology course. One reason often stated by students is that they are interested in people and in learning more about their society. Sociology is the discipline that allows students to study society using a scientific perspective. Sociology trains students to differentiate between common sense or biased ideas and valid sociological findings. Students are active participants in society and are constantly engaged in social interaction. However, their personal biases often influence their views of society. The mass media (television, newspapers, and magazines) report daily what is happening in U.S. society. Columnists and others sometimes attempt to predict future changes, such as what the family will be like ten years from now or how many people will be victims of AIDS; or they attempt to interpret why more people are using "pleasure drugs" such as cocaine or crack. Very often these interpretations are also highly subjective and based on the journalist's own biases or values. Many students may not know the difference between subjective and objective interpretations. Sociologists use methods that are different from those of journalists and people not trained in sociology.

Some students think that sociology is mostly common sense. They are unaware of the methods that sociologists use to arrive at scientifically based observations, and they don't know how to distinguish between personal beliefs and the social reality as uncovered by scientific investigation. For example, let us say that one day in class there is a discussion on drug abuse. One student states that he or she knows someone who uses crack and then proceeds to discuss the subject as if that acquaintance were representative of all crack users. Obviously, the student is not an expert on the subject. In fact, because of his or her limited range of experience, he or she may have many misconceptions about crack users and the effects of crack.

PERSONAL ISSUES AND SOCIAL ISSUES

Very often when students are asked to think of social issues or problems, they think of a personal problem that affects a friend or a family member: for example, Uncle Joe is an alcoholic, Cousin Mary suffers from depression, or a friend at school is flunking English. If a significant number of people in the society are affected by these types of problems (alcoholism, mental illness, course failure) and the public considers these issues to be of concern, then these issues are also social problems. But not all personal problems are social problems. For example, society may not be interested in your friend's failure, but if large numbers of college students are unable to pass freshman English, then this may become an issue of public concern.

As another example, consider Uncle Joe's drinking problem. Alcoholism is clearly a social issue since it directly or indirectly affects many people in the society. The problem is not simply an individual or family problem. Alcoholism is associated with spouse and child abuse, drunk driving, disorderly conduct, industrial accidents, and homelessness. The health care system must provide treatment for alcoholics. Communities must establish programs and shelters for indigent alcoholics. The criminal justice system must deal with alcohol-related criminal behavior. Lastly, the public through their taxes must pay for these programs.

In many instances, an individual problem may be part of a larger social phenomenon that is called a *social issue*. Sociologists study these social issues. A scientific study of alcoholism would not be based on personal knowledge of one person, as in the case of the student, or on interviews with several alcoholics, as might be the case in a journalistic interview. The sociologist would collect data on a representative sample of users. *Representative* means that the sample would include the full range of alcoholics, people from all parts of the United States and all walks of life. Based upon the study of this representative sample, the sociologist would then begin to make observations about alcohol abuse. The study of alcoholism is a continuing process. As science progresses, ideas are constantly being challenged, and many new ideas that were once accepted as facts are replaced by new ideas. New research may prove old ideas false, and this motivates the continuing search for more accurate knowledge.

THE STUDY OF SOCIOLOGY

Sociology is the scientific study of human social behavior. It involves the use of scientific methods to arrive at knowledge in a way similar to that of the natural and physical sciences. Sociology, however, is different from the natural and physical sciences in that people are both the researchers and the objects of research. Chemists may investigate the interaction of hydrogen and oxygen molecules, but it is highly unlikely that they will become emotionally involved with either type of molecule.

The subject matter of sociology, on the other hand, may cause subjective problems for the researcher. Specifically, personal bias may enter in since the subject matter of sociology frequently has high emotional content. For example, issues such as crime, drug abuse, abortion, and poverty may all lead to heated arguments and debates. Sociologists are not immune to this emotionality. It is very important for sociologists to become aware of their own personal feelings so that they can be more objective in their research and in their interpretations.

As a sociology student you will become involved in the process of scientific investigation. You will come to look at things that you previously took for granted in new and unexpected ways. Indeed, some ideas and concepts that you have accepted all your life may be challenged. You will gain new insights into the workings of your society and the social issues that face it. In fact, sociology has been called a "debunking" science because it has a tendency to contradict many everyday assumptions that people hold about their society. For example, some people believe that honest or dishonest persons can be spotted just by looking at them. But ask any store owner who has taken a bad check if he or she believes this. Scientific social research has demonstrated that physical characteristics are not related to moral temperament. You cannot "tell just by looking." Criminal behavior is much more complicated than many people believe. It involves many economic, sociological, and psychological variables. Facial characteristics are of little consequence in determining or predicting criminal behavior.

SOURCES OF DATA

This book offers you the opportunity to examine some of the critical social issues of the day. In so doing, you will be able to compare *your* everyday assumptions of social life with the best available scientific data. The data you will be using in your analysis will be from regularly published statistical sources. The U.S. Bureau of the Census is the major source of nationwide data. Besides publishing statistical reports based upon the decennial census (i.e., the census done every ten years), the bureau also publishes *The Statistical Abstract of the United States* every year. This source provides a wealth of statistical information ranging from the output of U.S. farms to changes in the Consumer Price Index. Other national data sources are also available. For the module on juvenile delinquency, you will make use of data from the Federal Bureau of Investigation's *Uniform Crime Reports*. This is the major source for nationwide crime statistics in the United States.

These are some of the sources you will be using in these modules. These and other sources of statistical data are available in most university libraries and in many local public libraries. After completing these modules, we hope that you will feel better equipped to undertake statistical research on your own. We also hope that you will value the contribution that such research can make to an accurate understanding of our social world.

THE FEAR OF STATISTICS

You may already have doubts as to whether or not you really want to work with statistics. One student fear that seems to be almost universal is "math anxiety." Many U.S. students appear to have an almost irrational fear of numbers. The mere mention of the word *statistics* can strike fear in the heart of many a student. In this book you will be asked to make use of and analyze statistical information. Do not panic. As you will see, the bark of statistics is worse than its bite. You will come to find that simple statistical analysis is exactly that: simple. At the same time, you will learn why statistics is an extremely useful tool. You will also discover how some of the statistics reported by the mass media are often misinterpreted.

For example, on television you may hear that car theft is a major problem in this country. In order to support this statement, FBI statistics are cited showing that a car is stolen every twenty seconds. Does this mean that right now, instead of worrying about the statistics in this book, you should be worrying about your car? These modules will teach you how to interpret statistics of this sort. You will also become better able to determine whether or not other people's interpretations of statistics are valid. Best of all, the kind of analysis you will be doing will be similar to the kind that is done by professional sociologists.

BASIC STATISTICAL TOOLS

Throughout this book you will be using simple descriptive statistics such as averages, proportions, ratios, percents, and percent change. Let us quickly review some of these items.

Averages

You use averages every day. For example, you hear sports fans talking about batting averages of their favorite players or weather forecasters speaking of the average rainfall in a particular month in your locale. Certainly most college students are concerned with their grade point averages. An average is a useful tool by which to summarize a mass of data. For example, it would be difficult or impossible for people to visualize whether or not April was an exceptionally wet month if weather forecasters did not use averages. In sociological research, three types of averages are often used: mean, median, and mode.

- *Mean:* The mean is the arithmetic average or the sum of a set of numbers divided by the total number of occurrences. In all likelihood you have calculated means since second or third grade. Remember the Friday morning spelling tests. If you wanted to know how well you were doing you would compute your average or mean score. For example, if you had five spelling tests and your grades were 100, 80, 90, 50, 70, you would add all your scores (100 + 80 + 90 + 50 + 70) to get the total (390). Then you would divide the total (390) by the number of tests (5) or 390/5 = 78.

- *Median:* Government agencies often make use of medians when speaking of such things as family income. Simply stated, the median is the middle number in a set of numbers arranged in order of size from largest to smallest or smallest to largest. The median cuts the set of numbers in half, so that half the numbers fall below the median and half above it. If we look again at our spelling test example, to calculate the median we would arrange the scores in order of size as follows: 100, 90, 80, 70, 50. The score in the middle is 80. There are two test scores higher than 80 and two lower than 80.

- *Mode:* The mode is not used very often. The mode is the number in a set of numbers that occurs the most frequently. Again, looking at the spelling example, we see that there is no mode, because no number occurs more than once. However, if instead of a 50 you had scored another 70, then there would be two 70s and 70 would be the mode.

Proportions and Percents

Proportions and percents are useful for making comparisons. Suppose you want to compare the number of females in your sociology class to the number in your history class. Your sociology class has 40 students, and 20 are females. Your history class has 100 students, and 50 are females. If you just state that your sociology class has 20 females and your history class has 50, it would be very confusing. It might give the impression that history is a subject that attracts more females than sociology. What causes the confusion is that the two class sizes are different. One way to standardize is to use a proportion. In other words, compare one part to the whole: i.e., how many females are there compared to the total number of students? For the sociology class, you would have 20/40 or 0.5, and for history, you would have 50/100 or 0.5. In this way you would see that both classes have the same proportion of females. To get a percent, multiply the proportion by 100. In this instance, if you multiply 0.5 by 100, you get 50 percent. You are really standardizing the number. Percent means per 100. In other words, if you had 100 people, how many would be females? This is a very useful statistic, because now you can make comparisons between groups of numbers when the sample size or base numbers are different.

Ratios

It is also useful to compare different parts to the whole. For example, if your sociology class has 20 females in a class of 40 students, then 20 of these students must be males. Now you can compare the ratio of females to males. There are 20 females to 20 males or 20/20. Reducing the fraction you get 1/1 or one female for every male. Suppose another sociology class of 40 has 16 females; then the number of males would be 24. The ratio of females to males would be 16/24 or 2/3 or 2 to 3. There are often set conventions for stating ratios. For example, sex ratios are usually given as males to females. In the modules, when you are asked for a ratio make sure you express the ratio in the manner it is asked for.

Percent Change

Often you will want to compute change over time: for example, the percent change in the number of smokers in your college from 1980 to 1998. Suppose your college had 600 smokers in 1980 and in 1998 had 100. In 1998, there are 500 fewer smokers. Let 1980, the initial time, be T_1 and let 1998, the final time, be T_2. The formula to calculate the percent change is expressed as follows:

$$\frac{T_2 - T_1}{T_1} \times 100 \text{ or}$$

$$\frac{1998 \text{ smokers} - 1980 \text{ smokers}}{1980 \text{ smokers}} \times 100 \text{ or}$$

$$\frac{100 - 600}{600} \times 100 = -83\%$$

This statistic means there was an 83 percent decline (note the minus sign) in the number of smokers between 1980 and 1998.

CONCLUSION

Now you are ready to begin your analysis of some social issues. The issues included for study in this book are all relevant and topical. Almost every day you hear or read about one of the issues discussed in the book. After completing each of the modules, you will be able to analyze more easily what you hear on television and read about in the newspaper. You will also be able to compare what everyone is saying about the issue with what you have discovered to be the objective facts. As an educated adult, you will develop a critical eye, learning not to accept at face value everything you hear and read. In addition, these modules will give you the opportunity to *apply* the concepts and theories you have learned in your sociology class and in assigned readings. We think you will find that doing these modules is not only fun but personally rewarding. You may even get enthusiastic about the endless fascination of "doing" sociology, motivated by the desire to better understand our social world and that most fascinating of all subject—ourselves.

MODULE 1

WHERE WILL YOU BE LIVING IN FIVE YEARS?

Push On—Keep Moving—THOMAS MORTON

People seem to be constantly on the move. Think for a moment how often you see moving vans on the road. Are so many people actually changing their addresses? Where is everyone going? Sometimes our general impressions of the world are not validated by the actual data, but this is not one of those cases. People in the United States are indeed on the move. Within any five-year period, about one third of the population moves.

People move for personal reasons. Some may decide to move because of employment opportunities. Others may wish to live in a warmer or a colder climate. Some may wish to be nearer certain relatives or they may wish to be farther away from certain relatives. Regardless of the specific causes, the amount of movement in this country is substantial.

Although large numbers of people change addresses, many are not changing the types of communities they live in. City dwellers tend to move to other cities. Suburbanites tend to move to other suburbs.

Because so many people move, demographers (social scientists who study population composition and change) have come up with precise definitions regarding the movement of people. A *migrant* is someone who moves from one county to another. In order to be officially listed as a migrant you must cross a county boundary line (which can also include crossing a state line, of course). Not everyone who moves crosses county lines. Sometimes people move across the street or around the corner. The Census Bureau utilizes the word *mover* to describe such a person. *Immigration* constitutes a move across a national boundary line: that is, from one country to another.

Because large scale migration does occur, a number of different groups in our society may be interested in knowing who is moving where. For example, politicians are very concerned with where people are moving. Both President

Bill Clinton and his Vice President Al Gore are from southern states. President Clinton was governor of Arkansas, and Vice President Gore was a senator from Tennessee. Southern states are very important in presidential elections because of the size of their populations. They are getting larger due to the migration to the "sunbelt" region of the country. This means that future presidential elections will also hinge on this "southern strategy." In addition, because of the large number of people living in suburban areas, candidates will concentrate a substantial part of their campaign schedule on these suburban populations.

This movement or migration of people is nothing new. The United States has a long tradition of people migrating from one area of the country to another. What groups of people might be concerned with changes in population size and composition? Think of your own community. Why would the migration of people be of interest to certain types of people in your community?

GOVERNMENT LEADERS

If large numbers of people are moving into a certain area, local officials will have to respond to this change by making important decisions. Questions concerning housing, health care, education, and police and fire protection will begin to emerge in areas of rapid population growth. Some of the questions would be:

- Should we build more schools?
- Do we have enough hospital or health care facilities to serve our growing population?
- Are there adequate public services (police, fire, sanitation) to serve our expanding community?

In an area of declining population the situation would be the reverse. Local officials would consider which facilities or services should be reduced rather than expanded.

BUSINESS LEADERS

Making a profit is a major concern of all business leaders. In addition, managers try to run their companies as smoothly and as efficiently as possible. Population movement can directly affect the functioning of any business. The potential pool of employees or potential consumers of the products or services offered, the ability to raise capital, and the availability of land are all related to changes in migratory patterns. If large numbers of people are moving into an area, a business leader may be concerned with the following questions:

- What age groups are moving into my area? (Should I invest in diaper services or nursing homes?)
- What is the marital status of the people moving in? (Should I build singles' clubs or nursery schools?)
- Are the people moving into the area professional or blue-collar workers? (Should my construction firm build office buildings or factories?)

If an area is beginning to experience declining population, this too is a concern to business leaders. Questions arise as to whether or not to close down the factory or sell the store. Is it time for the business to relocate? These are just a few of the basic questions related to migration that are important to business leaders.

YOU

Sometimes when we talk about people or groups on the move, we forget that we are really talking about individuals. Although it is historically correct to say that groups of people have been forced to move (Jews in Nazi Germany, Asians in Uganda, Native Americans in the United States), most people in the United States who move do so of their own free will. Why do individuals decide to move? There are many factors that can influence this decision. Among these are employment opportunities; a desire to be nearer certain family members or to seek a change in one's lifestyle; health reasons; a desire for a warmer or colder climate; life-cycle change (retirement, marriage, first major job, birth of a child); and a desire to find a place that feels comfortable, a place to call "home."

When analyzing why people move, demographers often talk about push-pull factors. *Push factors* are the reasons why someone leaves an area. For example, religious persecution and high unemployment are push factors. *Pull factors* are the reasons why people are attracted to certain areas. Pull factors include employment opportunities and religious freedom. Note that in our examples of push-pull factors, both practical concerns (employment) and ideological concerns (religious freedom) may be important to migration.

SOCIETY

The movement of people has a major impact on society in general. We are all affected by migratory patterns. For example, congressional representation is based upon population. If you live in an area that is losing population, your area may lose seats in the House of Representatives. Conversely, if you live in an area increasing in population, the number of seats in the House of Representatives may be increased. Also, this will affect the number of electors a state has in a presidential election. Thus, as people move around the country there may be shifts in centers of power. Traditionally the cities had the largest number of residents, and the representatives of these areas were able to wield a certain amount of power. Now this pattern appears to be changing, with more people moving to suburban and nonmetropolitan areas. The representatives of these areas now wield greater power.

From the societal perspective, migration may also affect the distribution of a society's resources (new housing, industry, etc.). If large numbers of people move from one area to another, the area of origin (where people move from) may lose jobs, skilled workers, and the need for housing may decline. The area of destination (where people move to) may gain in job opportunities, and the construction industry may begin to flourish. The area of origin will lose its economic vitality while the area of destination will experience a period of economic growth. The entire distribution of wealth in a society can be altered in this process. In sum, we can say that migration patterns affect society, government leadership, business leaders, and you, the individual member of society.

SOCIAL ISSUE

Where will you be living in five years? Let us examine some general data on geographical mobility. Then, we will be able to analyze the impact that mobility has on society in general and on each of us as individuals.

ANALYSIS

1. Table 1.1 presents some recent data on interregional migration.

Using the data provided, calculate the net migration for each region. Net migration is the difference between the in-migration and out-migration. You figure this by using the following formula:

In-Migrants − Out-Migrants = Net Migration

2. Which region is experiencing the greatest growth? _____

3. Which region is experiencing the greatest decline? _____

TABLE 1.1   Interregional Migration: 1994

| | Migration (in thousands) | | |
	In-Migrants	Out-Migrants	Net Migration
Northeast	348	676	_____
Midwest	706	737	_____
South	1,336	960	_____
West	746	763	_____

Source: *Current Population Reports*, P. 20, No. 485, August 1995.

4. Table 1.1 gives you an idea of the extent of mobility in one year. The Census Bureau also develops data that make projections for the future. Table 1.2 presents data on what the population distribution of the United States may be like in the year 2000. Calculate the percent change between the years 1993 and 2000 for each of the regions shown. Utilize the following format to calculate your answers.

$$\frac{\text{Year 2000} - \text{Year 1993}}{\text{Year 1993}} \times 100 = \text{Percent Change}$$

Example: Northeast

$$\frac{46,401 - 51,355}{51,355} \times 100 = {}^{-}9.6 \text{ percent}$$

Place your answers directly on the table in the column *Percent Change.*

TABLE 1.2   Resident Population (1,000) and Projections: 1993-2000

Region	Year		Percent Change 1993-2000
	1993	2000	
Northeast	51,355	46,401	_____
Midwest	61,070	59,714	_____
South	89,438	98,828	_____
West	56,044	62,519	_____

Source: *Statistical Abstract of the United States: 1993* Table 31, p. 28; *Statistical Abstract of the United States: 1994* Table 26, p. 27.

5. Which region will experience the greatest growth? Why do you believe this region will experience the greatest growth?

6. Which region will experience the greatest decline? Why do you believe this region will experience the greatest decline?

7. Now that we have examined the general mobility patterns, let us consider some of the factors that may motivate people to move to particular areas. Table 1.3 presents data on personal income by region. Calculate the percentage increase for each area in the space allotted in the table.

TABLE 1.3   Median Income of Households by Region: 1993–1995

Region	1993	1995	Percent Increase 1993–1995
Northeast	33,747	36,111	_____
Midwest	31,400	35,839	_____
South	28,441	30,942	_____
West	33,739	35,979	_____

Source: *Current Population Reports*, P60, No. 193, September 1996.

8. Which region has the largest increase? _____

9. Which region has the smallest increase? _____

TABLE 1.4   Annual Income and Expenditures for all Consumer Units: 1994

Region	Average Money Income of Households[1]	Total Expenditures	Discretionary Income
Northeast	45,319	32,565	_____
Midwest	39,442	30,335	_____
South	38,249	30,086	_____
West	45,284	35,368	_____

Source: *Statistical Abstract of the United States: 1996*, Table 705 and Table 712, p. 463; pp. 454–5.
1. For the year 1993.

10. Table 1.4 presents data on annual income and total expenditures by region. Calculate the discretionary income by region. Discretionary income is the money that remains after all expenses are paid.

11. Which region has the most discretionary income? _____

12. Which region has least discretionary income? _____

13. Which region do you believe will attract the most migrants in the next ten years? Why?

14. What impact do you believe this may have on the country as a whole?

15. Based upon the data in Tables 1.3 and 1.4, which region would you find most attractive? Why is it the most attractive?

16. What factors would you consider important in deciding where you would want to settle?

17. Where do you think you will be living in five years? Why?

MODULE 2

WHO'S BRINGING UP THE CHILDREN?

The little world of childhood with its familiar surroundings is a model of the greater world. The more intensively the family has stamped its character upon the child, the more it will tend to feel and see its earlier miniature world again in the bigger world of adult life.—CARL JUNG

Train up a child in the way he should go; and when he is old, he will not depart from it.—PROVERBS, 22:6

The traditional image of the U.S. family of the 1950s was a married couple with two or more children. The husband was the breadwinner and the wife was a full-time housewife and mother. TV shows such as "Father Knows Best" and "Leave It to Beaver" reflected that tradition. The family was the key factor in the socialization and the rearing of the children. Mom was an ever present figure in children's lives. When children came home from school, they were greeted by Mom with milk and cookies. She listened intently to their tales of the day's events and was there to comfort, encourage, and share in the trials and tribulations of childhood.

Today the image of the family that we see on TV is very different. There are a variety of family forms. A large number of family sitcoms feature white and African American single-fathers who are divorced or widowed. In "The Tony Danza Show," Danza portrays a divorced sportswriter raising two daughters. In "The Tom Show," Tom Armoss plays a divorced father with two daughters who has recently gone through an acrimonious divorce from his wife, Maggie, a TV talk show host. In "The Gregory Hines Show," Hines is a widower who has begun dating again and can relate first-hand to his twelve-year-old son's angst about dating for the first time. The show "Malcolm and Eddie" features two children of divorced parents. Romance revolves not only around the secret dating of Malcolm's father and Eddie's mother, but also on the competition between Malcolm and his gay sister for the same date. Homosexuality also becomes an issue in the long-running popular sitcom "Home Improvement," which is based on a more traditional two-parent family. In one episode a member of the cast comes out of closet. "Murphy Brown" continues to be popular with TV watchers. The controversy surrounding the network's decision to have the star of the show portray a highly successful TV newswomen who opts to have a child out of wedlock has largely disappeared.

Newspaper and magazine articles discuss issues such as unwed mothers, divorce, stepparenting, working mothers, latchkey children, and whether or not gay couples should be allowed to adopt. Stepfamilies or blended families, dual-career families, single-parent families, and gay families are now featured.

These changes reflect structural changes in the society and in the family. Today the traditional family with the husband as breadwinner and the wife as a full-time homemaker with two or more children is no longer the norm and comprises only a minority of families. In 1950 only 24 percent of wives in two-parent families worked. In 1995 only 23.8 percent of wives in two-parent families with children ages six through seventeen years were full-time housewives. Over 59 percent of married women with children under one are working. Today dual-career families are the norm. Divorce is also fairly common. It is projected that one in two marriages will eventually end in divorce. Remarriages, today, result in many blended families. Thirty-one percent of families with children are single-parent families and 85 percent of these are headed by females. Today there is a diversity of family patterns and lifestyles, and this will continue to be the norm in the future. The traditional family of the 1950s will be seen as one of many alternative types of families and as one that is suitable only for parents with young children. The concept of child-mother dependency is being replaced by the concept of early independence. The majority of children today do not come home from school to be greeted by mother. Many children come home to empty houses, go to after-school day care or babysitters, or attend other after-school activities. These activities fulfill two needs of the modern parent-supervision and training of the child.

The need for day care and before- and after-school care continues to be a growing concern in many communities. The demand for such programs often exceeds the supply. The quality of these programs varies from community to community. The effect of these programs on children is becoming more and more important as children's lives become more structured and controlled by adults other than their parents.

Even the leisure activities of children have changed. In the 1950s children often had hobbies such as model airplane building or stamp collecting or reading. TV and video games are the new leisure activities.

Children of the 1950s were encouraged to be children and to spend time developing at their own pace in unsupervised play. In the past, neighborhood children in their free time gathered in the street or in someone's yard or in a vacant lot to play such games as baseball and football. Today, children's play has been transformed from informal games to highly organized sporting events. Adults now organize and direct most sports programs for children, from Little League baseball to youth soccer. Today these programs mirror professional teams. Children's lives in the 1990s are very different from children's lives in the 1950s.

Children today are being socialized more by the community or society at large than in the past. In a number of communities, sex education, for example, is now seen as part of the school curriculum rather than the private domain of the family. More and more, parents are relying on teachers, coaches, babysitters, and others outside the family to help in the raising of their children. Kenneth Keniston compares the new parenting role to that of an executive. He states that "parents today have a demanding new role choosing, meeting, talking with, and coordinating the experts, the technology, and the institutions that help bring up their children."

Sometimes there is little coordination among parents, school officials, and others who are responsible for the children. As a consequence, some children are being neglected or left to rely on their peers rather than their parents for advice and counsel.

There are many variables that affect family life and childhood. Think of all the different variables that might affect childhood socialization patterns. Marital status, for example, would be one such variable. Are the parents divorced or separated? Is one parent deceased? Is the mother a teenage unwed mother? Another variable might be family size. Is the child an only child or does he or she have brothers and sisters? The type of community (whether the family lives in an urban, suburban, or rural area) will affect the lifestyle. Income level will also determine lifestyle and will be associated with age of marriage, size of family, child-rearing philosophies, and leisure activities.

In this exercise you will examine a few of the current trends that are reshaping family life and childhood.

SOCIAL ISSUE

Who's bringing up the children? The assumption has always been Mom, but is that true today? What has happened to women's roles as full-time housewives and mothers? Today, the majority of married women are working outside the home. Many children are growing up in single-parent homes. Children are spending less time with their parents. A 1985 study estimated that U.S. parents spend an average of seventeen hours a week with their children. How has this change affected the rearing of our children? Are teachers, coaches, peers, babysitters, and TV stars the new role models for our youth? Before you begin to answer these questions, it is important to define the term *children*. For this analysis, children are defined as youth between the ages of birth to eleven years.

This exercise is designed to help you answer the question, Who's bringing up the children? You will examine data on marital status, labor force participation, child-care arrangements, and TV viewing patterns.

TABLE 2.1 Participation Rate in Labor Force of Single, Married, Widowed, Divorced or Separated Women with Children under 18 Years: 1970-1995

Status	Children under 6			Children 6-17 Only		
	Single	Married[1]	Other[2]	Single	Married[1]	Other[2]
Year 1970	(NA)	30.3	52.2	(NA)	49.2	66.9
1980	44.1	45.1	60.3	67.6	61.7	74.6
1990	48.7	58.9	63.6	69.7	73.6	79.7
1995	53.0	63.5	66.3	67.0	76.2	79.5

Source: *Statistical Abstract of the United States: 1996*, Table 626, p. 400.
[1]Husband present.
[2]Widowed, divorced or separated.

ANALYSIS

1. Examine Table 2.1 and calculate the percent of full-time housewives with children under six years of age in 1995.

Percent of Full-Time Housewives with Children under Six Years

Married women _____

Single women _____

Other _____

2. Was the image of a full-time mother at home accurate for 1995? Discuss.

3. Examine Table 2.1 and calculate the percent of full-time housewives with children under six years in 1970.

Percent of Full-Time Housewives with Children under Six Years

Married women _____

Single women _____

Other _____

4. In 1970, was the image of a full-time mother at home accurate? Why or why not?

TABLE 2.2   Percent Distribution of Principal Type of Child-Care Arrangements, Used by Employed Mothers for Children Under 5 Years: 1977 and 1993

	June 1977[1]	Fall 1993
Care in Child's Home	33.9	30.7
By Father	14.4	15.9
By Other	19.5	14.8
Care in Another Home	40.7	32.1
Organized Child-Care Facilities	13.0	29.9
Mother Cares for Child While Working	11.4	6.2
Other Arrangements	1.0	1.2

Source: *Statistical Abstract of the United States: 1993*, Table 610, p. 384; *Current Population Report* P70–53.
[1]Data only for two youngest children under 5 years of age.

5. If the majority of mothers are working, how are young children being cared for? Table 2.2 gives the principal types of child-care arrangements for working mothers with children under five years. Examine Table 2.2 and determine what percent of working mothers or fathers are caring for their own children under five.

	1977	*1993*
Mother	_____	_____
Father	_____	_____
Total	_____	_____

6. How many were being cared for in an organized child-care facility (day-care or preschool programs)?

1977   *1993*

_____   _____

7. How were the majority of children under five with employed mothers being cared for in 1993? Discuss.

8. What might be some reasons why more parents are using day care?

9. What might be some reasons why more fathers are providing day care for their children?

10. Children of ages six through eleven years are usually in school most of the day. Let us compose a hypothetical weekday schedule for children in first to sixth grades.

24-Hour Weekday Schedule for Children 6-11 Years

	No. of Hours
School 9 A.M. to 3 P.M.	_____
Travel time to and from school	_____
Meals (breakfast and dinner, one-half hour per meal)	_____
Sleep (9 P.M. to 7 A.M.)	_____
Number of hours free	_____

11. Of the free time, what activities might the child be engaged in? List some activities.

TABLE 2.3   **Average Number of Hours of TV Viewed per Week by Children Ages 6–11**

Year	Hours
1965	24h 38 min[1]
1995	21h 40 min

Source: *Television Nielsen Reports 1986*, P. 9; 1995 statistics from *1997 Information Please Almanac*, p. 747.
[1]Average number of hours and minutes.

12. One activity you may have listed is watching TV. In order to arrive at some idea of how many hours per day the average child between the ages of six and eleven watches TV, examine Nielsen's statistics on TV viewing in Table 2.3.

Calculate the average number of hours per day of TV watched by children ages six to eleven years for 1965 and 1995 and the change in number of hours from 1965 to 1995.

Average Number of Hours per Day of TV

Hours   *Change*

1965 _____   1965–1995 _____

1995 _____

13. What are some reasons that might account for the decreases in the average number of hours per day of TV viewed?

14. Look back at your calculations in question 10. If you subtract the average number of hours of TV watched per day in 1995, how many hours of free time are left?

_____

15. The Miller Lite Report on American Attitudes toward Sports in 1983 interviewed parents and found that 62 percent of parents said that their children participated in organized sports activities. List some other types of organized activities besides sports that children might be engaged in after school.

16. Educational activities such as reading and homework are also important. How much time is left in your hypothetical schedule for educational activities?

_____

17. How much time do you estimate children spend on this activity? What implications does this have?

18. Your hypothetical schedule is for weekdays. What types of activities might the child be engaged in on weekends? Discuss.

19. Based on your analysis, who would you say are the major role models for children ages birth to eleven years?

20. Is the image of mother bringing up the children accurate? Why or why not?

21. If you had a child under five, how would you like him or her to be cared for and why?

22. If you were to have children, what types of activities would you want them to participate in and why?

MODULE **3**

ARE TEENAGE OUT-OF-WEDLOCK BIRTHS A SOCIAL PROBLEM?

My mom said she wouldn't get me birth control because it was
the same as giving me permission to have sex. I guess she was
really giving me permission to have a baby.
—TIME, Dec. 9, 1985.

The stigma of out-of-wedlock births is largely gone today. And certainly no one would want to go back to an era in which innocent children were stigmatized for the faults of their parents. The days of "shotgun marriages" and parents forcing their unwed pregnant daughters to give up their children for adoption are past. The terms "illegitimacy" and even "born out-of-wedlock" are rarely used. Today the term single mother refers to unwed mothers as well as divorced or widowed mothers.

In the media, one reads about the "love children" of famous people. "Murphy Brown", the television program, depicts Murphy as an unmarried mother with a successful career as a TV newswoman. Sociology textbook chapters on the family discuss traditional two-parent, single-parent, cohabiting, and homosexual couples. The traditional intact nuclear family (husband, wife, and children) is no longer presented as the ideal type.

Yet, most children born to teenage single mothers will grow up in poverty, dependent upon welfare. Some of these children will suffer from being unwanted and neglected. For some, the cycle of welfare dependency will continue into the next generation, since teenage girls often repeat the sexual patterns of their mothers. The lives of born out-of-wedlock children will have little similarity to the "love children" of the rich and famous.

Most teenage pregnancies are unplanned, even though 93 percent of public high schools offer sex education classes.[1] Of these pregnancies about half result in live births, the other half are terminated by miscarriage or abortion. Today the majority of unwed mothers decide to keep their babies rather than put them up for adoption. As of 1996 many of these young mothers received financial help from the government in the form of Aid to Families with Dependent Children, Food Stamps, Medicaid, and subsidized housing. According to former Surgeon General Joycelyn Elders, in 1992, the goverment spent $34 billion on Aid to Families with Dependent Children, Medicaid, and Food Stamps.

Because of the large cost to the taxpayer, concern by politicians often focuses on financial issues rather than social ones. Issues of how to get absent fathers to pay child support and how to get welfare mothers off the public dole become primary.

Yet, the social costs may be even greater than the financial ones to the society. Many of these children will never participate in the American dream. A high percentage will drop out of school, become delinquent or abuse drugs. Columnist Mona Charen states that 60 percent of rapists, 72 percent of adolescent murderers and 70 percent of long-term prison inmates came from fatherless homes.[2]

In 1994 approximately 30 percent of births were to unmarried mothers. Harvard sociologist Lee Rainwater predicts that the number will be 40 percent by the year 2000.[3] Research indicates that children growing up in female-headed households are more likely to grow up in poverty, drop out of school, become involved in delinquency, and to have emotional problems than children from two-parent families.

Teenage out-of-wedlock births are a problem for the United States. Many of these teenage mothers, since they never finished high school, will be unable to find jobs and will end up on welfare. With limited education and few parenting skills many of these mothers will experience difficulty in raising their children. The problems their children will face will be further compounded by the fact that many will grow up in low-income neighborhoods with drug and juvenile gang problems. Many of these children will experience social adjustment problems and need the help of social services. Some may even become wards of the courts. All of this will place a financial burden on the government and, in turn, on the taxpayer.

In the past, teenage pregnancy was not as large a problem as it is today. This was true even though the number of births to teenage mothers was higher in 1970 than today. The reason is that in the past many teenage girls who became pregnant were married or got married because they became pregnant. Today, many unmarried girls who become pregnant are having their babies and opting to raise the child on their own without financial help from the fathers. Having a child while one is still in her teens can have long-term consequences for these mothers in regard to educational attainment, employment opportunities, and life chances. While unwed teenage motherhood does not condemn one to a life of dependence, there is little question that it places a difficult burden on those who are still quite young and unprepared to meet the responsibilities associated with taking on adult roles.

Unwed motherhood has become a topic of national politics. Welfare, welfare reform, and illegitimacy are topics that were hotly debated in the United States Congress in 1996. Congress, reacting to rising costs of welfare and the public's concern that the present welfare system creates dependency, passed the Personal Responsibility and Work Opportunity Reconciliation Act of 1996, which President Clinton signed. The new bill abolishes the federal program of Aid to Families with Dependent Children (AFDC). In place of AFDC the federal government will provide block grants to states to set up Temporary Assistance to Needy Families (TANF). Under these block grants, states can create their own programs to assist those in need. The only requirements are that the state programs contain work requirements and have a five-year lifetime limit on assistance for recipients. These two provisions are designed to force welfare recipients to take control of their lives. To assist parents in caring for their children more federal money is being allocated for daycare and for improvement in the enforcement of payment of child support by fathers. The new bill attempts to reconcile two different perspectives on how to resolve problems of illegitimacy and welfare dependency.

Some scholars and politicians utilize a structural approach. This approach argues that problems associated with illegitimacy and welfare are best solved by improving educational and employment opportunities for those segments of the population at greatest risk of becoming unwed teenage mothers.

Other scholars and politicians advocate a cultural approach. They argue that the values of some groups in society contribute to irresponsible behavior such as out-of-wedlock births. Therefore, it is necessary to change values. In this case, welfare for teenage mothers is construed as encouraging financial dependency and discouraging self-sufficiency. Eliminating AFDC, then, is a way to encourage teenage girls to stay in school and not have children until they can afford them. Eliminating welfare for unwed mothers under 18 might also be seen as a way to make the parents of these girls assume responsibility for their daughters' behavior.

The sociological approach would attempt to examine both the structural and cultural factors that contribute to unwed teenage motherhood. Some questions that might be posed are: Why are lower-class teenage girls more likely than middle-class ones to have a child out-of-wedlock? What are the values, attitudes, and beliefs of each group that might lead to unwed motherhood? Finally, the sociologist would be interested in developing social policies that might alleviate the problem of out-of-wedlock births.

SOCIAL ISSUE

Is the number of out-of-wedlock births in the United States increasing and is there a relationship between teenage single motherhood and welfare dependency?

TABLE 3.1   Percent of Live Births to Unmarried Mothers by Race of Mother, 1960–1993

Year	1960	1970	1980	1990	1993
Total	5.3	10.7	18.4	28.0	31.0
White	2.3	5.5	11.2	20.4	23.6
Black	N.A.	37.6	56.1	66.5	68.7

Source: *Statistical Abstract of the United States: 1996,* Table 98, p. 79.

ANALYSIS

1. Examine Table 3.1. From 1960 to 1993 what has been the percent increase in births for unmarried women overall? _____

2. In 1993 which racial group had the highest percent of births to unmarried mothers? State and give percent. _____

3. In 1993 which racial group had the lowest percent of births to unmarried mothers? State and give percent. _____

4. Using data from Table 3.1, complete Table 3.2.

TABLE 3.2   Percent of Births to Unmarried Mothers by Race

Year	1970	1993	Percent Difference
White	_____	_____	_____
Black	_____	_____	_____

5. Discuss the patterns you discovered in the data analysis completed in Table 3.2.

TABLE 3.3 **Percent of Live Births to Unmarried Mothers by Hispanic Origin, United States, 1992**

Hispanic Origin[1]	Percent
Mexican American	36.3
Cuban	20.2
Central & South American	43.9
Puerto Rican	57.5

Source: *Statistical Abstract of the United States: 1996,* Table 97, p. 78.
[1]Hispanic persons may be of any race.

6. Until recently there was no separate category for Hispanics. Hispanic births were recorded as white or black dependent upon race. Table 3.3 gives 1992 births for Hispanics. For out-of-wedlock births which Hispanic group had the:

Highest percent? _____

Lowest percent? _____

7. What might account for the differences in percent of out-of-wedlock births by Hispanics from different areas of origin?

8. The Census Bureau 1994 Annual Report titled "Marital Status and Living Arrangements" states that in 1994: 57 percent of black children, 21 percent of white children and 32 percent of Hispanic children were living with one parent who has never married. Based on this information and the data in Tables 3.1, 3.2 and 3.3, what do you think will be the future of the traditional two-parent birth family?

9. Data indicate that 75 percent of children in single-parent families experience poverty before age 11. Examine Table 3.4, Poverty Rates for Children 6 Years Old by Family Type, to determine if there is a relationship between marital status and poverty. Which type of household has the highest rate of poverty?

_____

10. Which type of household has the lowest rate of poverty?

_____

TABLE 3.4   Poverty Rates for Children 6 Years Old by Family Type: 1992

All Races	Poverty Rate
All Family Types	24.0
Married Couple	12.7
Single Parent	55.2
Mother Only	58.9

Source: *Statistical Abstract of the United States: 1994*, Table 729, p. 476.

11. What factors might contribute to the differences in the poverty rate by family type?

12. According to Table 3.5, which racial or ethnic group had the highest rate

of poverty for all family types? _____

13. For all races and ethnic groups, which family type had the highest rate of poverty? _____

14. For female-headed families (mother only) give the rates of poverty for:

Whites _____

Blacks _____

Hispanics _____

TABLE 3.5   Poverty Rates for Children 6 Years Old by Family Type and Race: 1992

Race	White (non-Hispanic)	Black (non-Hispanic)	Hispanic (both races)
All Family Types	14.4	50.7	44.0
Married couple	8.4	19.3	34.3
Single parent	42.2	67.5	65.5
Mother only	46.2	69.2	68.6

Source: *Statistical Abstract of the United States: 1994,* Table 729, p. 476.

15. What factors might account for the differences that you found in question 14?

TABLE 3.6 **Proportion of AFDC Recipients with a High School Diploma or Some College Education Among Women Who Gave Birth as Teenagers and Those Who Did Not**

Year	Women Who Gave Birth as Teenagers	Women Who Gave Birth at Age 20 or Older
1976	33.1	42.9
1980	38.2	50.7
1984	41.6	56.3
1988	41.6	59.3
1992	46.7	62.2

Source: *GAO/HEHS-94-115 AFDC Women Who Gave Birth as Teenagers,* p. 19.

16. Table 3.6 provides information on AFDC recipients from 1976 to 1992. Educational level is highly correlated with employment. Without a high school education it is very difficult to find a job. Examine Table 3.6. What percent of AFDC women who gave birth as teenagers had high school diplomas?

In 1976 _____

In 1992 _____

17. Now examine Table 3.7, which compares the percentage of families below poverty level by race and educational level of the householder 25 years or older. For all races what is the relationship between education and poverty?

TABLE 3.7   Percent of Families[1] Below Poverty Level by Race and Education in 1994

Race/Ethnicity	All Races	Whites	Blacks	Hispanics
Less than High School	24.8	20.8	40.1	38.0
High School Graduate	10.9	8.5	26.0	20.7
College Graduate	2.6	2.1	5.1	6.4

Source: *Statistical Abstract of the United States: 1996,* Table 739, p. 476.
[1]Householder 25 years or over.

18. For each educational level, which ethnic or racial group has the highest rate of poverty?

Level of Education	Group with Highest Poverty Rate
No diploma	_____
High school graduate	_____
College graduate	_____

19. What variables other than educational level might account for the differences in poverty rates for whites, blacks, and Hispanics?

20. What kinds of programs would you suggest to decrease the number of unmarried teenage pregnancies?

21. What kinds of programs would you suggest to decrease welfare dependency?

ENDNOTES

[1]Lee Smith, "The New Wave of Illegitimacy," *Fortune,* April 18, 1994.
[2]Mona Charen, "At War with Fatherhood," *The Hartford Courant,* Aug 12, 1994, G15.
[3]Daniel Seligman, "Back to Family Values," *Fortune,* Nov. 29, 1993.

MODULE **4**

ARE GENDER ROLES STILL SEX-TYPED?

The problem lay buried, unspoken, for many years in the minds of American women. It was a strange stirring, a sense of dissatisfaction, a yearning that women suffered in the middle of the twentieth century in the United States. Each suburban wife struggled with it alone. As she made beds, shopped for groceries, matched slipcover material, ate peanut butter sandwiches with her children, chauffeured Cub Scouts and Brownies, lay beside her husband at night—she was afraid to ask even of herself the silent question—"Is this all?"
—BETTY FRIEDAN, *THE FEMININE MYSTIQUE*

How bitter it is to be a woman. Nothing on earth is held so cheap.—FU HSUAN

Traditionally, U.S. society glorified the role of motherhood. Marriage and motherhood were viewed as bringing women ultimate fulfillment and bliss. All little girls were socialized from birth to play the roles of wife and mother. The woman who failed to marry and have children was to be pitied. An unmarried woman was viewed by many as being someone who had been rejected. The term *spinster* has a very different connotation from that of the word *bachelor*.

If a married woman remained childless, it was automatically assumed by many of her friends and acquaintances that there was something wrong, that there was some medical reason why the couple couldn't conceive. Neighbors or relatives might gossip about the possible causes of the couple's "affliction." The idea that childlessness might be voluntary was not even considered. People married to have children. Motherhood was supposed to be an exclusive and all-encompassing role.

In the idealized image of motherhood of the 1950s, the woman lived exclusively for her husband and children, was everything to everyone, and was endlessly self-sacrificing, loving, patient, understanding, and tender. She kept the perfect house, was the perfect hostess, and raised perfect children. Her entire life was devoted to the care and nurturance of all family members and her success was measured by her ability to fulfill this nurturing task. She lived vicariously through her husband and children. It was through this experience of being wife-mother that she was given a sense of self-worth. Whether she would be perceived as a good person or a bad person depended upon how well she fulfilled this role. If a woman felt unfulfilled or had aspirations for roles other than that of housewife and mother, she often was made to feel that she was maladjusted, that she was fighting her biological destiny. Biology and gender roles were seen as being directly related, and biology rather than culture was seen as dictating temperament and personality. Many women yearned for some sort of self-identity beyond that of being someone's wife and mother but they suffered in silence. Often these women did not understand why they couldn't find happiness in this role when other women did. Women who dared to break from tradition and work outside the home experienced pangs of guilt. They feared that they were different from other women; that perhaps they were selfish, and that they neglected their husbands and children. Friends and neighbors often reinforced these feelings by criticizing women who worked outside the home. If their children showed problems of adjustment, no matter how trivial (or even normal for that stage of the child's development), other parents, teachers, and relatives often pointed to the fact of the mother's employment as the reason for the problem.

The woman who desired a career often experienced a double bind. If she worked outside the home, she faced condemnation or censure by the community as well as personal feelings of self-doubt about whether or not she should work. On the other hand, if she stayed at home, she might feel guilty for not fulfilling her need to be something more than a housewife and mother. This dilemma was caused by the cultural forces prevailing at the time that shaped definitions of what were appropriate male and female roles.

In this traditional setting, family roles were based upon a sexual division of labor. Specifically, men were supposed to have the responsibility for the instrumental functions and women were responsible for the expressive functions of family. By *instrumental functions,* sociologists mean the so-called practical concerns of family life. These include supplying financial resources for the family (i.e., bringing home the paycheck), taking out the garbage, fixing the leaky roof, and other "manly" chores. The *expressive functions* involve the giving of emotional support and care, especially to the young.

During World War I and World War II some women departed from this traditional pattern of the family and entered the labor force. They took over many traditional male jobs because men were off fighting the war. However, once the war was over, women were expected to return happily to their full-time roles as housewife and mother. Women were expected to work outside the home only if it was necessary for the welfare of the country or their families, such as in wartime or because of economic necessity.

It was thought that the wife of a good husband and provider should have no desire to work. Her pleasure would come from being a good wife and mother. Although between the wars women were given the right to vote, it was assumed by many people that wives would automatically vote as their husbands did. Men made the major decisions. The image of what women should be like had changed very little.

Disillusionment with the traditional female role did not become a social issue until the early 1960s. The catalyst for this reexamination of traditional sex roles was the publication of Betty Friedan's book, *The Feminine Mystique*. The issue of appropriate roles for women became a public one and was given wide media coverage.

In addition, during the 1960s, the United States underwent an educational revolution. For the first time in the country's history large numbers of young people began to attend college. Traditionally, higher education had been seen as a predominantly affluent domain. Education was now viewed as the key to occupational success, not just a luxury for the upper classes. With this changing attitude toward higher education, and with more women going to college, the necessary link between employment and women's ability to compete in the marketplace was established.

The traditional dichotomy of sex roles was challenged. Many married women were successfully combining family and career, just as single women were finding fulfillment in their careers. More and more the concept of the traditional full-time mother as the only appropriate role for women was being questioned. The long-accepted image of male and female roles was being challenged. The mass media were quick to popularize the image of the liberated female. Television programs began to appear that portrayed women raising children alone ("Alice," "One Day at a Time"). These women not only raised their children without the help of a male, but they also held full-time jobs.

Some media coverage was hostile to this changing picture. Phyllis Schlafley became a popular spokesperson for this antichange perspective, warning that the role of full-time mother was being threatened by the Women's Liberation Movement. Because the traditional family was considered a sacred social institution, changes in the family structure were seen by some as dangerous and even immoral.

Numerous articles, both pro and con, about women in nontraditional roles were published. Frequently, the image of the modern woman was contrasted with that of the traditional woman. Men in nontraditional roles were also discussed in the press.

Today most parents want their daughters to pursue a career. Little girls grow up expecting to have both a family and a career. The traditional roles of male as breadwinner and female as wife and mother have changed.

Employment is a key variable for understanding the changing roles of men and women in U.S. society. Occupation and income are two variables that are very important in determining one's status in U.S. society. Are women entering the labor market primarily in traditional types of female employment such as secretaries, nurses, and elementary school teachers, or are they also attaining positions in traditional male areas, such as doctors, lawyers, and engineers?

The number of women employed, as well as the type of employment, are two factors that will help you to analyze the change in male and female roles.

This exercise is designed to help you answer the following questions: What has happened to the role of women? Are women still predominantly housewives or have they become equal participants in the job market with men?

SOCIAL ISSUES

Are males and females still in sex-typed roles? Are women primarily housewives and men primarily breadwinners? If women work, do they work at so-called women's jobs?

You will examine labor force statistics on men and women to answer these questions. Four sets of data are presented: Labor Force Participation by Sex, Female Labor Force Participation by Marital Status, Male and Female Earnings, and Percent of Males and Females in Certain Occupations. Look over the tables and then begin the exercise. You will analyze what changes are taking place in the labor market in terms of the types of jobs and the incomes of men and women.

ANALYSIS

Are females primarily housewives and males primarily breadwinners? Examine Table 4.1 on page 37.

1. In 1980 what percent of males were employed? _____

What percent of females? _____

2. In 1990 what percent of males were in the labor force? _____

What percent of females? _____

3. In 1995 what percent of males were in the labor force? _____

What percent of females? _____

TABLE 4.1   Percent Labor Force Participation[1] by Sex: 1980–1995

	Year		
Sex	**1980**	**1990**	**1995**[2]
Male	77.4	76.4	75.0
Female	51.5	57.5	58.9

Source: *Statistical Abstract of the United States: 1996*, Table 615, p. 393.
[1]For civilian non-institutionalized population 16 years old and over.
[2]Not strictly comparable with previous years.

4. Now compute the differences in labor force participation for men and women for 1980, 1990 and 1995.

Percent Difference: Male-Female Labor Force Participation

	1980	1990	1995
Male-Female			
Difference	_____	_____	_____

5. Summarize the findings of the above calculations.

TABLE 4.2   Percent Females in Labor Force, Age 16 Years and Over by Marital Status: 1970–1995

	1970	1980	1990	1995
Marital Status				
Single	56.8	64.4	66.7	66.8
Married	40.5	49.9	58.4	61.0
Widowed, Divorced, or Separated	40.3	43.6	47.2	47.4

Source: *Statistical Abstract of the United States: 1996*, Table 625, p. 399.

6. Does marital status have anything to do with the employment status of women? In Table 4.2 examine the percentages of women employed by marital status between 1970 and 1995 and compute percent changes.

Marital Status: Percent Change in Number in Work Force

	1970–80	1980–90	1990–95	1970–95
Single	_____	_____	_____	_____
Married	_____	_____	_____	_____
Widowed, Divorced, or Separated	_____	_____	_____	_____

7. What patterns can you discern from the above calculations?

TABLE 4.3 Median Income for Year-Round Full-Time Workers by Sex: 1970–1994

Sex	Year	
	1970	1994
Male	19,173	31,612
Female	11,591	23,265

Source: *Statistical Abstract of the United States: 1993*, Table 728, p. 465; *Statistical Abstract of the United States: 1996*, Table 725, p. 469.

8. Examine Table 4.3 to see if males and females received equal pay.

a. How much more money did males earn in 1994 as compared to their income for 1970? _____ How much more did females earn?

_____

b. What was the difference in income between males and females in 1970? _____ For 1994? _____

9. One way of analyzing differences in earnings is to calculate the proportion of earnings one group has to another. This is a simple calculation. In this case we wish to see how female earnings compared to male earnings. To find this percentage, simply divide the smaller number (female earnings) by the larger number (male earnings).

$$\frac{\textit{Female median income}}{\textit{Male median income}} = \textit{proportion of female to male earnings}$$

What is the proportion for 1970? _____

What is the proportion for 1994? _____

What is the difference in proportions for 1970 and 1994? _____

10. What do these figures tell us about changes in male-female earning differentials?

11. List some variables other than discrimination that might account for some of the earnings gap.

TABLE 4.4   Employed Persons by Sex and Occupation: 1972 and 1995

	Year			
	1972		1995	
Occupation	Male	Female	Male	Female
Accountants	78.3	21.7	47.9	52.1
Engineers	99.2	0.8	91.6	8.4
Lawyers and Judges	96.2	3.8	73.8	26.2
Physicians	89.9	10.1	75.6	24.4
Elementary Teachers	14.9	85.1	15.9	84.1
Librarians[1]	18.4	81.6	16.8	83.2
Registered Nurses	2.4	97.6	87.5	93.1
Secretaries	0.9	99.1	1.5	98.5

Source: *Statistical Abstract of the United States: 1980*, pp. 418-19; *Statistical Abstract of the United States: 1996*, Table 637, pp. 405–407.

[1]Includes archivists and curators.

12. Traditional female occupations in 1972 were elementary school teachers, librarians, nurses, and secretaries. Were these positions still predominantly female in 1995? What data from Table 4.4 can you cite to support your answer?

13. Were there any changes from 1972 to 1995? Compute percent differences in the number of males in these four traditionally female occupations.

Percent Male

	1972	*1995*	*Percent Difference*
Elementary Teachers	_____	_____	_____
Librarians	_____	_____	_____
Registered Nurses	_____	_____	_____
Secretaries	_____	_____	_____

14. Traditional male occupations in 1972 were in the areas of accounting, engineering, law, and medicine. Were these positions still predominantly male in 1995? What data can you cite to support your answer?

15. Were there any changes from 1972 to 1995 in the male occupations cited above? Compute the percent differences for females in these four traditionally male occupations.

Percent Female

	1972	*1995*	*Percent Difference*
Accountants	_____	_____	_____
Engineers	_____	_____	_____
Lawyers and Judges	_____	_____	_____
Physicians	_____	_____	_____

16. How would you describe the overall pattern that you found from Table 4.4?

17. What factors do you believe contribute to this changing pattern?

18. Given the data you have just examined, what projections might you make about the future of traditional sex-typed occupations?

19. When you graduate from college what kind of occupation would you like to have? Is this a traditional or nontraditional sex-typed occupation?

MODULE 5

IS AMERICA A DRUG CULTURE?

"O true apothecary! Thy drugs are quick."—SHAKESPEARE

Turn on the TV. What do you hear? Do you suffer from irregularity? Take this. Do you have a nagging headache? Try that. Feel tired, run down? This pill is for you. Can't sleep? Just pop this before you retire. Feel fine and have no health complaints? Don't be deluded by being symptom free. You need calcium supplements or super vitamins. There seems to be a drug for everything that ails you as well as drugs to keep you healthy and fit. The message seems to be that if you aren't taking any drugs, you may be abusing your body. Americans have become conditioned to believe that every ache and pain can be cured by some miracle drug and that in order to insure longevity and continued good health we need to take preventive measures.

Certainly, there is some basis for our belief in the power of drugs. Miracle drugs such as antibiotics, vaccines for polio, diphtheria, smallpox, and other diseases have all but eradicated many of the dread diseases of the world. No one today talks of having bubonic plague, the black death, or polio. Drugs have proven to be very important in modern society. Yet Americans tend to rely too heavily on drugs and too often abuse the very drugs that were designed to improve their health. People become addicted to valium and other tranquilizers and sleeping pills. Pain killers too often become addictive. Pep pills or amphetamines may be seen by some as giving the individual a competitive edge. Even when people relax and enjoy themselves, they often have a drink. Cocktail parties, champagne toasts at weddings, anniversaries, and other occasions are the norm in our society. A holiday ushers in good cheer, and good cheer has become synonymous with alcoholic beverages. No wonder, then, that alcohol is the most abused drug in our society.

Open your own medicine cabinet. What do you see? Aspirin, cough medicine, antacids, antiseptics for cuts, mouthwash, toothpaste, deodorant, and probably a few old prescriptions whose purpose is long forgotten.

Of course, you say these are legal drugs rather than illegal ones. The drug issue is not concerned with legal drugs, but the sale, use, and abuse of illicit drugs. Yet, drugs such as valium, alcohol, and morphine are legal and often abused. Today cocaine is outlawed, but years ago it was found as an ingredient in cola sodas. In fact, in the 1880s many of the patent medicines contained opiates. It wasn't until 1914, with the passage of the Harrison Act, that there were any laws prohibiting the sale and use of opiates.

New drugs are continually being added to the list of illegal ones. For example, marijuana was added in 1937 and LSD in the 1960s. At one time heroin was thought to be a panacea for morphine addiction. Synthetic drugs are often produced that mimic older illegal drugs in an attempt to escape the law or in the belief that they will be less addictive.

In a highly competitive, fast-paced society, people are often looking for ways to relax, let off tension, and escape pressure. Social drinking is one highly accepted means.

For a brief time, cocaine was seen as a nonaddictive, although illegal, party drug. But soon there were reports of respectable business people, lawyers, doctors, and entertainers who became dependent on the drug and squandered their earnings and careers. But the public was especially shocked when Len Bias, the 1986 NBA Celtic draft choice, who had a reputation for not using drugs, died of cardiac arrest brought on by cocaine use. Here was a twenty-two-year-old gifted athlete with a bright future who threw his life away.

"Coke" has also been blamed for a number of prominent celebrities' deaths. Film star River Phoenix; Robert F. Kennedy's son, David Kennedy; and star of "Saturday Night Live" John Belushi; all died of cocaine overdoses. Yet, some people continue to experiment with and use the drug.

Cigarette smoking was considered a benign and enjoyable social habit. It wasn't until fairly recently that the medical establishment linked smoking to cancer and heart disease. A once acceptable habit is now seen as harmful.

Part of our thinking about drugs is related to our knowledge of them and their effects on the body. For example, in the 1960s marijuana was touted as a drug with no serious side effects, which posed less of a threat to health than cigarette smoking or drinking. Only recently have the ill effects of marijuana been discussed. As society learns more about certain drugs, laws as well as public opinion change.

No segment of our society has been free of the abuse of drugs. For example, Olympic athletes have taken steroids, amphetamines, and other drugs in order to improve performance. Ben Johnson, the Canadian sprinter who set a world record in the 100-meter dash in the 1988 Olympics, was stripped of his gold medal after testing positive to anabolic steroids.

In 1990 Hulk Hogan of the World Wrestling Federation admitted that he used steroids to pump up his muscles. To thousands of children and their parents, Hulk was a positive role model. He was noted for telling his young fans to eat their vitamins and to say their prayers.

Drugs have been used by athletes to restore their bodies to a state in which they can play with injuries. Pain killers such as codeine and muscle relaxants are commonly used to enable athletes to continue to compete. Some cynical news columnists have referred to the new breed of athletes as "chemical heroes." Various sports commissions and boards are working to correct the problem. Many athletic heroes have been tarnished by drug problems. Anabolic steroid use is well documented as a problem in college, Olympic, and professional sports, However, a recent study indicates it is also a high school problem. In a survey reported in the *Journal of the American Medical Association,* 6.6 percent of boys in the twelfth grade in the United States admitted to using or having used anabolic steroids. Almost 58 percent indicated that they used steroids to enhance athletic performance or to prevent or treat injuries. What was surprising was that 26.7 percent said they used steroids to improve appearance and 35.2 percent of steroid users weren't involved in high school sports. The image of drug abuse as a lower-class problem has ceased to be a reality. No segment of society is free from the potential for the misuse of drugs.

Sales of drugs is big business. It is estimated that in 1990 Americans spent $40.4 billion on illegal drugs and $81 billion on alcohol and tobacco products.[1]

SOCIAL ISSUE

Is America a drug culture? How pervasive is drug use in U.S. society? Is drug use primarily a problem of youth or does it cut across age groups? Are there differences in use by sex? Are some drugs more popular than others? Is drug use declining? This exercise is designed to answer these questions. You will examine data on drug use by year and age.

ANALYSIS

Drug use and abuse have often been seen as problems of the young. Many people believe that youth experiment with illegal drugs in defiance of parents and in rebellion against society. Marijuana, LSD, and cocaine are seen as being part of the so-called youth culture. Legal and socially acceptable drugs, such as alcohol, tranquilizers, and cigarettes, are considered part of the adult world, the older establishment, the generation of parents. Abuse of these drugs is more hidden because they are not considered illegal and therefore escape the onus of official police statistics.

[1]*1994 Information Please Almanac, P.* 6.

TABLE 5.1   Current User of Drug by Drug Type and Age Group, 1994

Type of Drug	Percent of Youth (12-17 years)	Percent of Young Adults (18-25 years)	Percent of Older Adults (26 years and older)
Marijuana	7.3	12.2	3.0
Hallucinogens	1.2	1.5	(B)
Cocaine	0.4	1.0	0.6
Tranquilizers[1]	0.2	0.4	0.1
Alcohol	16.3	63.8	55.6
Cigarettes	9.8	26.5	24.7

Source: *Statistical Abstract of the United States: 1996*, Table 221, p. 144.

Note: Statistics for heroin use not available.

[1]Nonmedical use.

B Base too small.

Examine the data in Table 5.1 on drug use by type of drug and age group to determine if the image presented is correct.

1. Do different age groups use different drugs? For each type of drug indicate which age group has the highest current user percentage.

Marijuana   _____

Hallucinogens _____

Cocaine   _____

Tranquilizers _____

Alcohol   _____

Cigarettes   _____

2. Based on your findings, is it true that youths and young adults have higher rates of drug use for illegal drugs than older adults?

3. Is it true that older adults have higher rates of legal drug use than younger adults and youths?

4. Marijuana has been described as the preferred drug of teenagers and alcohol as the preferred drug of their parents. Based on Table 5.1 how accurate is this image? Explain.

5. Now find out if there have been any changes in the types and amount of drug use since 1974. Has drug use decreased, increased, or remained about the same for illegal drugs? See Table 5.2. For each age group, calculate the percentage change in drug use and write it in the percent difference column in Table 5.2.

TABLE 5.2   Current User of Illegal Drugs by Age, 1974 and 1994

| Drug | Percent of Youths (12–17 years) | | |
	1974	1994	Percent Difference
Marijuana	12.0	7.3	_____
Hallucinogens	1.3	1.2	_____
Cocaine	1.0	0.4	_____

| Drug | Percent of Young Adults (18–25 years) | | |
	1974	1994	Percent Difference
Marijuana	25.2	12.2	_____
Hallucinogens	2.5	1.5	_____
Cocaine	3.1	1.0	_____

| Drug | Percent of Older Adults (26 years or over) | | |
	1974	1994	Percent Difference
Marijuana	2.0	3.0	_____
Hallucinogens	NA	(B)	_____
Cocaine	NA	0.6	_____

Source: *Statistical Abstract of the United States: 1996*, Table 221, p. 144.
B Base too small.

6. For youths (twelve to seventeen years) has drug use increased, remained about the same, or decreased? Explain.

7. For young adults (eighteen to twenty-five years) has drug use increased, remained about the same, or decreased? Explain.

8. For older adults (twenty-six years or older) has marijuana use increased, remained about the same, or decreased? Explain.

9. In the last few years there has been a nationwide effort to educate young people about the dangers of drug use. Examine the statistics in Table 5.3 to determine if drug use among high school seniors has changed since 1980. Calculate the percent difference in drug use from 1980 to 1995.

TABLE 5.3   Drug Use of High School Seniors: 1980 to 1995

High School Students	Percent Ever Used		'80-'95 Percent Difference
	Class of 1980	Class of 1995	
Marijuana/Hashish	60.3	41.7	_____
Hallucinogens	13.3	12.7	_____
Cocaine	15.7	6.0	_____
Crack	NA	3.0	_____
Heroin	1.1	1.6	_____
Sedatives	14.9	7.6	_____
Stimulants[1]	26.4	15.3	_____
Tranquilizers	15.2	7.1	_____
Alcohol	93.2	80.7[2]	_____
Cigarettes	71.0	64.2	_____

Source: National Institute on Drug Abuse/University of Michigan Institute of Social Research.
Reported in *The World Almanac and Book of Facts 1997*, p. 966.
[1]Nonmedical use.
[2]Data for 1995 not directly comparable to 1980.

10. Based on your calculations of percent differences in Table 5.3, what trend is occurring among high school students in regard to drug use? Explain.

11. What do you think are some of the reasons for this change?

12. What are the 3 most popular drugs used by high school seniors?

13. Although it is illegal to sell alcohol to youths under 21, most high school seniors report using it. What can be done to prevent alcohol use by high school students?

14. You probably do not consider yourself a drug user. However, can you think of any legal or illegal drugs that you have taken?

15. Do you think that advertisements for pain killers, sleeping pills, and other types of drugs have made you more accepting of drug use? Explain.

16. Drug abuse, both legal and illegal, is a major problem for not only high school students but for all age groups in the United States. What policies can you suggest to eliminate drug abuse?

MODULE **6**

TWO-FISTED JANE: MYTH OR REALITY?

…the emancipation of women appears to be having a twofold influence on female juvenile crimes. Girls are involved in more drinking, stealing, gang activity, and fighting—behavior in keeping with their adoption of male roles.
—FREDA ADLER, *SISTERS IN CRIME*

All-girl gangs made their debut in New York City while the "granny bashers" were terrorizing part of London with razor blades and knives.
—FREDA ADLER, *SISTERS IN CRIME*

Until fairly recently, delinquency was considered a male problem. Fist fights, gang wars, and vandalism were thought of as male activities. Boys who were delinquent were considered to be acting out male roles: as males, they were supposed to be daring, aggressive, and independent. This behavior was considered an excessive extension of appropriate male behavior. In addition, young males were expected to be mischievous. The phrase "boys will be boys" became an excuse for certain types of behavior that would not be acceptable if performed by adults.

Many boys modeled their behavior after the macho image of the tough, nonemotional male. Television, movies, and books all supplied models for this tough guy image. The cowboy taking on the bad guys or the cop chasing the crooks are two examples of rugged individualism, and in the movies, Arnold Schwarzenegger epitomized the traditional male.

In keeping with this image, many boys judged each other and themselves in terms of their ability to defend themselves and to have pocket money. Status and success were often measured in these terms. Therefore, fist fights and stealing, although illegal, were seen by some boys as activities supportive of the male role.

Girls, on the other hand, were expected to be demure, passive, and attracted to the opposite sex. They were expected to seek the attention of males. This female preoccupation was in keeping with what would be expected of them as adults: finding husbands and raising children. Even when females participated in delinquent acts, the types of acts that they engaged in were seen as reflecting this passive, dependent, female role. Female delinquency primarily involved running away from home, incorrigibility, and sex offenses (being sexually active as a juvenile). Most female delinquency was comprised of *status offenses* (offenses that would not be considered a crime if the girl were an adult). These offenses were seen as indicative of a poor family situation. Girls who ran away were thought to be having problems at home, especially in their relationships with their parents. Incorrigibility (or ungovernability) was also often viewed in terms of a girl's inability to adjust to her family situation. Delinquent girls were judged to be in need of supervision and guidance. If a girl engaged in stealing and other types of crimes, she was usually accompanied by a boy, and the boy was often held responsible for the girl's behavior. It was thought that girls needed protection rather than punishment. As with male role models in society, the mass media offered appropriate role models for female behavior. Female delinquents were a rarity on the television or movie screen.

Female delinquency, in general, was not considered a serious problem. It was felt that once the girl found a husband, she would settle down to raising a family and would no longer pose a problem to society.

Delinquency, then, was seen as primarily a male problem. The patterns of male and female delinquency were considered to be very different, because they paralleled the differences in male and female roles. For example, even when girls engaged in criminal behavior on their own, the arrest statistics indicated that the nature of the act reflected the female role. Girls who stole, for example, were involved primarily in shoplifting and rarely in car theft, which was a male domain.

Today in the United States cultural definitions of what is considered appropriate male and female behavior are changing. Girls are choosing to pursue occupational goals that were once considered appropriate only for males. Females are becoming more equal to males in occupational and social roles.

In the press there has been much discussion of women's liberation and the effect it is having on male and female roles. The macho male ideal is changing with expectations that men should be more emotional and nurturant than in the past. Male and female gender roles are becoming more similar. Some people, such as Freda Adler, see these changes in perception of what is appropriate female behavior as having an effect on female delinquency. She believes that females are becoming more violent as they adopt male roles.

The media have also reported increases in female crime and delinquency arrests, indicating that behind these dramatic cases is a general surge in crimes committed by women. In general, the public still seems to be much more astonished by the activities of female criminals than they are by the activities of male criminals.

SOCIAL ISSUES

Are females becoming more similar to males in their patterns of delinquency?

In order to determine whether or not this is true, you need to examine some national statistics. The best statistics available are arrest statistics, which show whether or not the individual accused of committing the crime is male or female. However, arrest statistics only tell us who gets caught. We still don't know exactly how many males and females actually committed criminal acts, since some did not get caught. In fact, it could be argued that the reason fewer girls have been arrested for certain offenses such as car theft is not that they steal fewer cars, but that they are cleverer than boys and avoid detection. We doubt that many of you would agree with this logic. It does, however, point out one limitation of arrest statistics: not everyone who commits a criminal act gets arrested. Arrest statistics, then, are only a rough indicator of the actual number of males and females committing these acts.

The best source of arrest statistics for the United States are the FBI *Uniform Crime Reports*. The Federal Bureau of Investigation (FBI) annually collects crime statistics from all the police departments in the United States. Although this is a voluntary reporting system, almost all of the departments report. These statistics are then compiled by the FBI into an annual report called the *Uniform Crime Report*. From the arrest statistics for males and females under eighteen, you can gain some idea of trends in arrests over time. Table 6.1 is adapted from the *Uniform Crime Reports* tables. It indicates the number of arrests for serious crimes of males and females under eighteen from 1970 to 1990.

The FBI classifies crime into two categories: serious crimes, Type I; less serious crimes, Type II. The Type I crimes comprise what is called a crime index. Murder, rape, robbery, and aggravated assault are on the violent crime index; burglary, larceny-theft, motor vehicle theft, and arson are on the property crime index. In 1979, arson was added to the property crime index. These are the offenses that are most often referred to in the news. For example, you may read in the newspaper that over the last year arrests for property crime rose 30 percent or that arrests for violent crime are down 10 percent.

So that you will have some idea of what types of crimes are included in each category, we have listed the FBI definitions of these crimes as stated in the *Uniform Crime Reports*. You may want to read through these definitions and look at the tables given in the exercise before beginning to answer the questions.

Definitions of Type I Offenses

1. *Criminal Homicide*—a. Murder and nonnegligent manslaughter: the willful (nonnegligent) killing of one human being by another. Deaths caused by negligence, attempts to kill, assaults to kill, suicides, accidental deaths, and justifiable homicides are excluded. Justifiable homicides are limited to: (1) the killing of a felon by a law enforcement officer in the line of duty; and (2) the killing of a felon by a private citizen. b. Manslaughter by negligence: the killing of another person through gross negligence. Excludes traffic fatalities. While manslaughter by negligence is a type I crime, it is not included in the Crime Index.

2. *Forcible Rape*—The carnal knowledge of a female forcibly and against her will. Included are rapes by force and attempts or assaults to rape. Statutory offenses (no force used—victim under age of consent) are excluded.

3. *Robbery*—The taking or attempting to take anything of value from the care, custody, or control of a person or persons by force or threat of force or violence and/or by putting the victim in fear.

4. *Aggravated Assault*—An unlawful attack by one person upon another for the purpose of inflicting severe or aggravated bodily injury. This type of assault usually is accompanied by the use of a weapon or by means likely to produce death or great bodily harm. Simple assaults are excluded.

5. *Burglary-Breaking or Entering*—The unlawful entry of a structure to commit a felony or a theft. Attempted forcible entry is included.

6. *Larceny-Theft (except Motor Vehicle Theft)*—The unlawful taking, carrying, leading, or riding away of property from the possession or constructive possession of another. Examples are theft of bicycles or automobile accessories, shoplifting, pocket-picking, or the stealing of any property or article which is not taken by force and violence or by fraud. Attempted larcenies are included. Embezzlement, "con" games, forgery, worthless checks, etc., are excluded.

7. *Motor Vehicle Theft*—The theft or attempted theft of a motor vehicle. A motor vehicle is self-propelled and runs on the surface and not on rails. Specifically excluded from this category are motorboats, construction equipment, airplanes, and farming equipment

8. *Arson*—Any willful or malicious burning or attempt to burn, with or without intent to defraud, a dwelling house, public building, motor vehicle or aircraft, personal property of another, etc.

Definitions of Selected Type II Offenses

1. *Prostitution and commercialized vice*—Sex offenses of a commercialized nature, such as prostitution, keeping a bawdy house, procuring, or transporting women for immoral purposes. Attempts are included.

2. *Drug abuse violations*—State and local offenses relating to narcotic drugs, such as unlawful possession, sale, use, growing, and manufacturing of narcotic drugs.

3. *Drunkenness*—Drunkenness or intoxication. Excluded is "driving under the influence."

4. *Runaways*—Limited to juveniles taken into protective custody under provisions of local statutes.

TABLE 6.1 Juvenile Arrest Trends by Sex: 1970-1990

Offenses Charged	Males under 18		
	1970	1990	Percent Change
Murder & nonnegligent manslaughter	1,072	1,895	+76.8
Forcible rape	2,380	3,585	+50.6
Robbery	23,737	19,822	-6.5
Aggravated assault	13,421	35,421	+163.9
Burglary	97,200	87,390	-10.1
Larceny-theft	157,911	222,711	+41.0
Motor vehicle theft	50,633	52,396	+3.5
Arson[1]	—	5,150	—
Crime Index Total	346,496	1,082,609	+212.44

Offenses Charged	Females under 18		
	1970	1990	Percent Change
Murder & nonnegligent manslaughter	80	108	+35.0
Forcible rape	—	66	—
Robbery	1,813	1,675	-7.6
Aggravated assault	2,265	6,178	+172.8
Burglary	4,450	7,818	+75.7
Larceny-theft	56,009	88,143	+57.4
Motor vehicle theft	2,784	6,539	+134.9
Arson[1]	—	555	—
Crime Index Total	63,243	322,423	+409.8

Source: *Uniform Crime Reports: 1970* (Washington, D.C,: FBI, U.S. Department of Justice), Table 26, p. 124; *Uniform Crime Reports: 1990*, Table 28, p. 179.

[1]Arson was not listed as an Index Crime until 1979.

Now examine the data in Table 6.1. What types of comparisons of male and female arrests can be made from the data given? Probably, the first thing you thought of was a comparison of the change in the actual numbers of arrests for males and females from 1970 to 1990. These statistics are referred to as volume statistics. *Volume statistics* give frequencies of arrests. Volume or frequencies are difficult to visualize. For example, if arrests for murder increased from 100 to 110, is that more or less of an increase than an increase in arrests for robbery from 1000 to 1100? Differences in volume would indicate an increase of 10 arrests for murder and 100 arrests for robbery. At first glance it may appear that the increase in arrests for robbery is much greater than for murder. However, the proportional increase is the same. For both offenses there have been 10 more arrests for every 100 arrests. 100/1000 = 10/100 or 10 percent. In order to compare increases and decreases per 100 arrests, percents are often used. This allows us to compare increases or decreases based on a standard base figure. However, this change in the number of people arrested is not necessarily the result of an increase in criminality among the populace, or even an increase in the number of acts committed. The number of people detected by the police may have increased or the size of the population may have changed. For example, if the size of the population increased and the proportion of people arrested for criminal acts remained the same, volume statistics would indicate an increase in arrests. To illustrate, let's say that in 1970 there were five arrests for murder in a town of 100,000. In 1980 there were six arrests in the town, whose population had grown to 120,000. The number of arrests for murder has obviously increased. However, the rate of arrests has remained the same. In other words, there were five arrests per 100,000 people or one arrest for every 20,000 people in 1970. In 1980, there were six arrests per 120,000 people or one arrest for every 20,000 people. The rate of arrests is the same, because between 1970 and 1980 the total population increased by 20,000 people.

Using a ratio is another statistical comparison that is helpful in comparing overall changes in male and female arrests. A sex ratio would compare the number of male arrests to female arrests. For example, if ten males and five females were arrested for robbery in one year, the ratio of male to female arrests would be ten to five or 10/5, which reduces to 2:1 or two male arrests for every one female arrest. By using volume, percent, and ratio statistics we can gain a more exact picture of the changing relationship between male and female delinquency. The following exercise will ask you to make comparisons in volume, percent, and ratio of arrests for juvenile males and females for the ten-year period from 1986 to 1995.

TABLE 6.2 Juvenile Arrest Trends by Sex for Violent Crimes: 1986–1995

Offenses Charged	Males under 18			Females under 18		
	1986	1995	Percent Change	1986	1995	Percent Change
Murder and nonnegligent manslaughter	1,170	2,245	+91.9	85	138	+62.4
Forcible rape	3,928	3,769	−4.0	66	84	+27.3
Robbery	23,848	37,978	+59.3	1,759	3,863	+119.6
Aggravated assault	27,593	46,695	+69.2	5,005	11,418	+128.1
Violent Crime Index Total	56,539	90,687	+60.4	6,915	15,503	+124.2

Source: Adapted from *Uniform Crime Reports: 1995* (Washington, D.C: FBI, U.S. Department of Justice), Table 33, p. 213.

ANALYSIS

---

1. Refer to Table 6.2. Have the number of arrests for violent crimes by juveniles increased in the last ten years?

2. It is estimated that the population of the United States in 1995 was 176,320,000 and in 1986 161,254,000. Calculate the percent increase in population.

3. Compare the percent increase in juvenile violent arrests to the population increase. Which is increasing at a faster rate?

4. Based on your answer to question 3, does it appear that juveniles are becoming more violent?

5. Now examine Table 6.2. Which sex has had the greatest percent increase in arrests for violent crimes?

6. What are the percent changes in arrests for females for these offenses?

	Percent Change
Murder & nonnegligent manslaughter	_____
Forcible rape	_____
Robbery	_____
Aggravated assault	_____

7. From the percent change statistics does it appear that girls are becoming more violent? Why or why not?

8. What other statistical comparisons could be made?

9. If a journalist stated that female and male increases in arrests for violent crimes are now similar, would this statement give a false picture of female involvement in crime? Why?

10. In order to gain a more accurate picture of whether or not females are becoming more violent, you should also look at volume statistics: the actual
numbers of males and females being arrested. Complete the table below.
(Refer to Table 6.2)

Offenses Charged	Males			Females		
	1986	1995	Changes in Number of Arrests	1986	1995	Changes in Number of Arrests
Murder	_____	_____	_____	_____	_____	_____
Forcible rape	_____	_____	_____	_____	_____	_____
Robbery	_____	_____	_____	_____	_____	_____
Aggravated assault	_____	_____	_____	_____	_____	_____

11. Now examine total number of arrests for each offense. Who had the most
arrests for the offense over the ten-year period, males or females?

Greatest Number of Arrests

	1986	1995
a. Murder	_____	_____
b. Rape	_____	_____
c. Robbery	_____	_____
d. Aggravated assault	_____	_____

12. Now compute ratios of male to female arrests for each offense by year.

$$\frac{\text{Number of males arrested}}{\text{Number of females arrested}} = \text{M/F ratio}$$

	1986	1995
a. Murder M/F Ratio	_____	_____
b. Rape	_____	_____
c. Robbery M/F Ratio	_____	_____
d. Aggravated Assault M/F Ratio	_____	_____

13. Have the ratios increased or decreased? Discuss each one separately. Explain what is meant in each case by the statistics. In other words, if the 1986 male/female ratio for murder was 14:1, what does the number 14:1 really mean? Then, compare the ratio for 1986 and the ratio you calculate for 1995. Discuss the change.

a. Murder

b. Rape

c. Robbery

d. Aggravated assault

TABLE 6.3   Arrests for Self-Destructive Offenses by Sex for 1995

Offenses Charged	Males Under 18	Females Under 18
Prostitution	570	466
Drug Abuse	116,627	16,696
Drunkenness	12,009	2,243
Runaways	74,713	101,657

Source: Adapted from *Uniform Crime Reports: 1995* (Washington, D.C.: FBI, U.S. Department of Justice), Table 33, p. 213.

14. From your calculations, are Adler's and the media's perceptions accurate that girls are becoming more violent than in the past? Discuss.

15. Now let's look at some offenses that are seen as less serious to the society and may be categorized as self-destructive (as shown in Table 6.3).

For the offenses listed in Table 6.3 indicate who had the greatest numbers of arrests, males or females?

Greatest number of arrests

a. Prostitution   _____

b. Drug abuse   _____

c. Drunkenness   _____

d. Runaways   _____

16. Now calculate the ratios of male to female arrests for each offense.

$$\frac{\text{Number of males arrested}}{\text{Number of females arrested}} = \text{M/F}$$

a. Prostitution   _____

b. Drug abuse   _____

c. Drunkenness   _____

d. Runaways   _____

17. Are females more likely than males to commit self-destructive offenses? Explain.

18. Based on arrest statistics for violent and self-destructive delinquency patterns are there still basic sex differences? Is male delinquency a more serious problem than female delinquency? Discuss your overall findings and conclusions.

19. From personal experiences in junior high school and high school was male delinquency a more or less serious problem than female delinquency? Explain.

MODULE *7*

DOES IT PAY TO GO TO COLLEGE?

Education is the best provision for old age.—ARISTOTLE

Why go to college? Isn't it true that some plumbers and electricians who don't go to college make more money than a lot of college graduates? Is it really true that you will make more money if you go to college? Or are you wasting four years sitting in class? Maybe you have had second thoughts about your college education, especially if you have been studying late and thinking about some of your high school friends who are now working and who may have more free time and more money than you do.

Even though you may have had these thoughts, you decided to attend college. Your decision was no doubt influenced by your parents and teachers, who told you that college would enrich your life in a variety of ways. For example, a college education helps individuals to expand their knowledge. It gives them a broader sense of the world they live in. It exposes them to new ideas and new ways of thinking. A college education may impact on individuals in a variety of ways, although the idea of a financial reward for going to college is usually a very powerful incentive.

Economic mobility in U.S. society is largely tied to education. In a highly technological society, specialization and expertise in a given field have become very important. All the indications are that the importance of technological expertise will continue in the future. In U.S. society, social class is determined primarily by educational attainment and occupational status, and one's occupation usually determines one's income. There is strong evidence that we are moving toward becoming a society that will be divided into two distinct classes: there will be one class of highly skilled individuals and another class of people with few, if any, skills. The rewards of society (power and wealth) will go to the skilled workers.

Both you and your parents are probably making a financial sacrifice in order for you to attend college. This sacrifice includes not only the cost of going to college, but also the loss of income you might have earned if you did not go to college. And the expense of a college education is constantly rising. Colleges, like individuals, are affected by inflation. Just as an individual family may have to pay more for heating oil and electricity, so too do colleges and universities. These costs are passed along to the students and are reflected by the rising cost of tuition. In the fall 1997 semester, the cost of tuition, room, and board for a student to attend an elite private university such as Harvard was $30,080. For an out-of-state student to attend a public university such as the University of Connecticut, the cost was $19,222. For an in-state student, the cost was $10,704. If inflation continues, these tuition costs will be an even greater burden than they are now.

Congress in 1997 in an effort to make a college education more affordable for low and middle income students included a tuition tax credit in the tax reform bill. The bill allows a student or his or her parents to claim an annual Hope tax credit of up to $1,500 toward what was paid for tuition and fees the first two years of college. After that, a Lifetime Learning Credit of $1,000 a year, rising to $2,000 in the year 2003, can be claimed. To qualify for the maximum credit, an individual must have an adjusted gross income of less than $40,000 or a couple less than $80,000. Some financial advisors fear that students may never see the savings, because colleges will adjust financial aid packages.

Sociologists often use the *deferred gratification pattern* concept to describe behavior in which people sacrifice present rewards for a potentially richer future. They are referring to working for long-term goals with future payoffs rather than for short-term goals with immediate payoffs. Deferred gratification means that people are investing in their future. The assumption is that future rewards will be substantially greater than the immediate ones. The deferred gratification pattern is seen by sociologists as a middle-class phenomenon. Research indicates, however, that members of all social classes are aware of the importance of college. Unfortunately, out of financial necessity many working- and lower-class parents have traditionally encouraged their children to be self-supporting as soon as possible.

Obviously, the choice of whether or not one goes to college is based on more than a financial decision. Even if one could earn as much or more after attending a trade school, one might still want to get a college education and become a high school teacher. Rewards other than financial often govern our behavior. Self-fulfillment and enjoyment in a job are also important. By the same token, one may decide to get a college education and go into a trade.

Whether or not one would like to go to college, however, the decision about whether it is possible to do so may be based on financial considerations. Today, because the cost of a college education has risen so rapidly, many working- and lower-class parents who would like their children to go to college may not have the necessary financial resources. Thus, the decision about whether or not a child goes to college may be based more on the financial situation than on the deferred gratification pattern. College may still be more of an option for middle-class children than for working-class children. But, because of changes in federal allocation of funds for education, even middle-class families may have difficulty sending their children to college.

This discussion, then, raises two questions. One, are middle-class children still more apt to go to college than lower-class children? Two, does a college education pay off financially? This exercise is designed to investigate these questions.

SOCIAL ISSUE

Does everyone have an equal opportunity to go to college? Does it pay to go to college?

ANALYSIS

First, let's determine if everyone has an equal opportunity to go to college. One major variable relevant to this question is the cost of a higher education. Table 7.1 compares the average costs of a higher education for both public (state, county, and city colleges and universities) and private institutions.

1. Calculate the average yearly cost (tuition, room, and board) for attending public and private colleges or universities and the difference in cost between public and private institutions.

TABLE 7.1   Average College Costs for Resident Undergraduates at 4-Year Colleges by Type of School: 1990–1995

	Public		Private	
Year	Tuition & Required Fees[1]	Room and Board[2]	Tuition & Required Fees	Room and Board
1990–91	$2,035	$3,289	$10,348	$4,750
1994–95	$2,982	$4,100	$14,510	$6,500

Source: *Statistical Abstract of the United States 1996*, Table 290, p. 187.

[1]For in-state students.

[2]Beginning in 1987, rates reflect 20 meals per week, rather than meals served 7 days a week.

Average Yearly Cost of Attending College 1990–91 and 1994–95

	Public	Private	Difference
1990–91	_____	_____	_____
1994–95	_____	_____	_____

2. Briefly describe the differences in cost for public and private colleges for 1990–91 and 1994–95.

3. If public institutions are less expensive than private, what are some reasons why some students elect to go to private rather than public institutions?

4. Table 7.1 shows that the cost of a higher education has risen substantially from 1990 to 1995. Calculate the percent change in costs.

Percent Change in Cost

Years	Public	Private
1990–1995	_____	_____

5. Briefly summarize the changes you have noted above.

6. What factors do you believe have contributed to the rising cost of a higher education?

7. Table 7.2 presents data on full-time college enrollment of 18- to 24-year-old dependent family members. Young adults who are out on their own are not included in these data. Calculate the percentage of these students who attend college for each income level, and for both sexes.

8. Which group has the lowest percent of enrollment?

for males _____   for females _____

9. How do the patterns of enrollment differ for males and females? What might account for the differences you note?

TABLE 7.2 Full-Time College Enrollment of Primary Family Members 18 to 24 Years Old By Family Income, and Sex: October, 1995

Income Level	Male		Female	
	Number in College (1,000)	Percent	Number in College (1,000)	Percent
Less than $10,000	107	_____	91	_____
$10,000–$19,999	140	_____	151	_____
$20,000–$29,999	193	_____	343	_____
$30,000–$39,999	253	_____	267	_____
$40,000–$49,999	218	_____	223	_____
$50,000–$74,999	568	_____	582	_____
$75,000 and over	792	_____	721	_____
Not reported	276	_____	264	_____
Total	2,547	_____	Total 2,642	_____

Source: *Current Population Reports*, P20–492, October 1995 (Update), Table 15, pp. 61–62.

10. How is the variable of income related to the ability of young people to enter college?

11. What other variables besides income do you think are associated with whether or not a person attends college?

12. Does everyone have an equal opportunity to go to college?

TABLE 7.3   Mean Money Earnings (in 1996 Constant Dollars) for Year Round, Full-Time Workers, Aged 25–34, by Sex and Educational Attainment: 1995

Year of School Completed	Male	Female
9th–12th Grade (No diploma)	19,996	14,154
High School Graduate	24,558	17,985
Some College	27,295	22,160
Bachelor's Degree	38,033	30,750
Mean	$39,047	$26,214

Source: *The Condition of Education 1997/Supplemental...or Higher, by Sex and Race/Ethnicity: 1970–1995;*
http://www.ed.gov/NCES/pubs/ce/c9733d01.html

13. Table 7.3 represents data that will help you to answer the question, Does a college education pay off financially? What variables are given in the table?

14. What is the difference in mean income between the lowest and highest educational groups?

For males _____

For females _____

For which sex is the differential greater? _____

15. According to the table, how much more on average does a college graduate with four years of college earn than a high school graduate?

For males _____

For females _____

16. College graduates earn approximately what percentage more in income than high school graduates?

For males _____

For females _____

17. What factors might help explain the differences in the income data for males and females?

18. Does it pay to go to college? Explain.

19. What factors made you decide to go to college?

20. What advantages do you think a college education will give you? Explain.

MODULE **8**

ARE WE STILL A NATION
OF IMMIGRANTS?

Remember, remember always that all of us, and you and I es-
pecially, are descended from immigrants and revolutionists.
—FRANKLIN D. ROOSEVELT, 1938

The United States has a long history of being an immigrant nation. From its earliest beginnings, large numbers of settlers arrived from different nations and colonized the new world. After the Revolutionary War and the establishment of the United States as an independent nation, one of the major needs of the new country was for more people. In the colonial and postcolonial periods the country was very underpopulated. So from its earliest beginnings the United States encouraged immigration and saw itself as a nation of immigrants.

The earliest immigrants arrived from western and northern Europe. Specifically, large numbers of newcomers came from the British Isles, France, and the Netherlands. Many of these people came seeking religious freedom. In addition, large numbers of forced immigrants came from Africa as slaves. During the early and mid-nineteenth century, immigration patterns shifted slightly and large numbers of new arrivals came from Ireland, Germany, and the Scandinavian countries. During the latter part of the nineteenth century and early part of the twentieth century another shift in immigration occurred and large numbers of immigrants came from southern and eastern Europe. These new immigrants came in large numbers and differed from the earlier immigrants in that many of them were either Catholic or Jewish. Many came from Italy, Russia, and Poland. Today, immigrants are still arriving on our shores, but their cultural backgrounds are different from the earlier immigrants. Today many of the new arrivals are coming from Latin America and Asia.

Throughout the history of immigration, there have been people who have been opposed to an open immigration policy. The term *nativist* may be applied to these individuals and groups who claim that America is for Americans. On the other hand, there have always been groups who have favored continued immigration.

Wherever the immigrants' area of origin, once in the United States questions arose about their ability to assimilate into the mainstream of U.S. society. *Assimilation* is a process by which new groups enter and become absorbed into the society and culture of their new homeland. For some immigrants, the process can be relatively easy. For others it may be quite difficult. There are several factors that contribute to the ease or difficulty of this transitional process.

If the incoming group is very large, assimilation is usually slowed for several reasons. First, if the group is large, the native population (those people who are already residing in the society) may feel threatened by their presence. The fear that they are being taken over may be shared by many and xenophobia can develop. *Xenophobia* is a fear of anything foreign. Second, if the group is large it may retain its own cultural identity and may develop its own social institutions in the new land. These social institutions would parallel those of the mainstream society. For example, if the group is large enough, they may settle in their own distinctive neighborhoods, supply their residents with social services, and even develop their own educational institutions.

A second factor that may influence the speed of the assimilation process is the cultural distinctiveness of the new group. If the new group is very different from the dominant group in the new society, there will be greater difficulty in being accepted. In the past, people from Africa, Asia, and southern and eastern Europe faced the most opposition to their assimilation into U.S. society, although in varying degrees. If there are differences in skin color, religion, cultural practices, and language, greater problems in the assimilation process may emerge.

A third factor in predicting the ease of assimilation is related to the economy of the host society and the economic traditions of the incoming group. If the immigrant group is made up of large numbers of poor and uneducated people (as was often the case in the past) then they may face substantial opposition to their assimilation. Ideas may develop among the native population that these poor newcomers will not be able to contribute to society and in fact may become a burden on the society. If the immigrant group is largely middle class they may have an easier time in the assimilation process. One should be cautious, however, for in a number of instances middle-class minorities also face prejudice and discrimination because of fear of economic competition. Jews in the West and the Chinese in Asia are both examples of this type of immigrant group.

A fourth factor contributing to the ease or difficulty of assimilation does not have to do with the immigrant group itself but with the nature of the economy of the host society. If the host society is going through a period of economic expansion, immigrants may be accepted more easily because they fill the labor needs of the expanding economy. On the other hand, if the economy is going through a period of inflation and/or high unemployment then immigrants will be seen as competitors for scarce resources and they will not be welcomed.

A variation of this theme is occurring in the United States today. While the United States has experienced economic expansion in the 1980s, the economic expansion is of a different sort from the past. Most modern industrial economies are based upon a need for highly skilled workers. Many unskilled and semiskilled jobs of the past are now done by machines. Therefore, while there may be an increase in the number of jobs available in the labor market, the jobs require a higher degree of training and technological expertise. Jobs requiring unskilled or semiskilled workers are also increasing; however, these positions are found in relatively low-paying service-oriented industries (i.e., busboys in restaurants). The image of the poor immigrant worker landing on these shores and entering the labor force at the lowest end of the ladder and then climbing the ladder of success may be more difficult to assess today. The current U.S. economic system is much more complex when compared to the economy of 100 years ago. The path earlier immigrants took on their road to success is not necessarily the same path recent immigrants will travel.

This module will give you the opportunity to analyze immigration patterns in the United States. However, it should be noted that we will not deal with undocumented (illegal) aliens or refugees. After having analyzed the data, you will be able to see to what degree the United States is still a nation of immigrants.

SOCIAL ISSUE

Are we still a nation of immigrants? How have patterns of immigration changed over time? What impact does this immigration have on U.S. population trends?

ANALYSIS

1. Have there been changes in where our immigrants are coming from? Examine the immigration data in Table 8.1. Included in the table are data from the 1970s and for the most recent year for which we have data. Calculate the percentages for each area of origin.

2. In order to get a clearer picture of the changing immigration patterns, fill in the blanks on p. 82 using data from Table 8.1.

TABLE 8.1   **Immigrants (in thousands) by Area of Origin: 1971–1980, 1996**

Area of Origin	Year			
	1971-80		1996	
	Number	Percent	Number	Percent
Europe	801.3	_____	147.6	_____
Asia	1,633.8	_____	307.8	_____
North America	1,645.0	_____	340.5	_____
South America	284.4	_____	61.8	_____
Africa	91.5	_____	52.9	_____
Other	37.3	_____	5.3	_____
Total	4,493.3	_____	916.0	_____

Source: *Immigration to the United States in Fiscal Year 1996.*

Percent Difference in Immigrants by Area of Origin: 1971-80, 1996

Area of Origin	Year (in Percent)		Percent Difference
	1971-80	1996	
Europe	_____	_____	_____
Asia	_____	_____	_____
North America	_____	_____	_____
South America	_____	_____	_____
Africa	_____	_____	_____
Other	_____	_____	_____

3. Which area of origin has the greatest percent increase in immigrants?

_____

4. Which area of origin has the greatest decline? _____

5. Table 8.2 presents data on immigrants by specific countries. Calculate the percent each country contributes to the total number of immigrants.

6. Using the data in Table 8.2, list the countries by area and calculate the percent.

Caribbean (and Latin America)		Asia	
Country	Percent	Country	Percent
_____	_____	_____	_____
_____	_____	_____	_____
_____	_____	_____	_____
_____	_____	_____	_____
Total	_____	Total	_____

TABLE 8.2   Immigrants Admitted by Selected Country (in thousands): 1996

Country	Immigrants Admitted	
	Number	Percent
Mexico	163.6	_____
Philippines	55.9	_____
India	44.9	_____
Vietnam	42.1	_____
China	41.7	_____
Dominican Republic	39.6	_____
Cuba	26.5	_____
Ukraine	21.1	_____
Russia	19.7	_____
Jamaica	19.1	_____
Total (All Countries)	916.0	_____

Source: *Immigration to the United States in Fiscal Year 1996.*

7. What general statements can you make about the patterns you observe in question 6?

TABLE 8.3   **Immigrants Admitted by Metropolitan Area of Intended Residence: 1991**

Metropolitan Area of Settlements	Number
New York	133,168
Los Angeles–Long Beach	64,285
Miami	41,527
Chicago	39,989
Washington, DC–MD–VA	34,327

Source: *Statistical Abstract of the United States: 1993*, Table 10, P. 12.

8. What percent of all immigrants are settling in these five metropolitan areas?

9. Where are the immigrants settling? Examine the data in Table 8.3. What do all five major areas of settlement have in common?

10. What percent of all immigrants are settling in Los Angeles? _____

11. Why do you believe the Los Angeles area accounts for such a high percentage?

12. What percent of all immigrants are settling in New York? _____

13. Why do you believe New York accounts for such a high percentage?

14. In general, is it fair to say we are still a nation of immigrants? Explain.

15. Do you know who from your family was the first to immigrate to the United States? How do you believe this person felt about his or her immigration experience? If the person is still alive, you may wish to interview him or her.

MODULE 9

DOES EQUALITY EXIST IN AMERICA?

We are all equal, but some are more equal than others.
—UNKNOWN

Prejudice—Weighing the facts with your thumb on the scales.
—LEON AIKMAN

Racism is an ideology or belief system that tries to legitimate the dominant position of a group. Historically, racism supported the idea that Americans whose ancestors came from northern and western Europe were superior to Americans whose ancestry was of southern and eastern European, Asian, or African origin. This sense of superiority included notions of superior temperament and superior intelligence. In the eighteenth and nineteenth centuries, racist ideas were used to legitimate slavery. After the Civil War, when slavery was outlawed, southern states passed a series of Jim Crow laws that in effect kept black Americans "in their place." These laws, too, were supported by racist ideology.

Racist ideology was not something that existed solely in the South, however. Northern whites also believed in the concept of racial superiority. Instead of creating Jim Crow laws, the northern states practiced racial segregation. African Americans were excluded from certain residential areas, and they were not allowed to participate in a number of occupations. Even recreational areas were segregated. Discrimination was widespread throughout the United States.

African Americans in the South also attended separate facilities. The difference was that segregation in the South was backed by law, while in the North it was supported by custom. In the South there were separate parks, stores, movie theaters, and schools. Segregation in the South was rationalized by the excuse that although the facilities for blacks and whites were separate, they were equal. The rhetoric and the reality were very different, however. Black facilities were underfinanced and understaffed. The poor quality of the public school system prevented blacks from getting an adequate education, thus limiting them to low-paying, menial jobs. Evidence indicates that African Americans were subjected to inferior facilities of all sorts. The term *separate* was used as a cover for what was really discrimination.

In order to maintain this discriminatory system, African Americans were not allowed to participate in the political system. Through a variety of mechanisms, including the threat of violence and actual violence, blacks were kept away from the polls. As a result, blacks did not have access to any positions of power or influence in U.S. society. Without this access to power there was no opportunity to change the system of separateness and discrimination.

The terms *prejudice* and *discrimination* are often used to explain the conditions just described. Prejudice and discrimination are deeply rooted in U.S. society. Although the terms are often used interchangeably, they have different meanings. *Prejudice* is an attitude; it involves beliefs and feelings of a negative nature toward a particular group. Because prejudice is internal to the individual, it is impossible to see and very difficult to study. *Discrimination,* on the other hand, involves behavior. Discrimination may be defined as treating people differently because of the group they belong to. This differential treatment is readily observed; attitudes are not.

The civil rights movement developed because some people began to challenge the traditional treatment of African Americans in U.S. society. The modern civil rights movement began in 1954 with the Supreme Court decision that the "separate but equal" doctrine was unconstitutional. That decision, given in the case of *Brown* versus *the Board of Education of Topeka, Kansas,* resulted in the beginning of the desegregation of the U.S. public school system. It was argued that segregation was harmful to both black and white children, and the idea of separation itself was condemned as discriminatory.

The civil rights movement of the late 1950s and 1960s was a social movement designed to eliminate racial discrimination. It was felt by many that if discrimination were eliminated, attitudes would also change. The Montgomery bus boycott of 1955, the freedom rides in 1961, and the sit-ins in the early 1960s were organized efforts to bring pressure to eliminate discrimination. Groups such as the NAACP (National Association for the Advancement of Colored People), SNCC (Student Nonviolent Coordinating Committee), and CORE (Congress of Racial Equality) worked to bring pressure for social change.

The Civil Rights Act of 1964 was designed to bring about legislative changes that would dramatically change black and white relations in the United States. In many respects this legislation was seen by many as a way of bringing about a social revolution. By outlawing discrimination, it was hoped that racial prejudice would also diminish and eventually disappear. The Civil Rights Act of 1964 provided greater protection of voting rights, barred discrimination in all public facilities, gave the federal government power to intervene in school desegregation cases, and outlawed discrimination in the work place.

Even though the Civil Rights Act of 1964 outlawed most major forms of social discrimination, does equality between racial groups now exist in the United States?

Before you begin to examine this social issue, an additional word on terminology. Throughout the module the terms *black* and *white* are used to designate Americans of African ancestry and Americans of European ancestry. However, we want the reader to be aware that both terms mask the diversity that exists within each category. People labeled black may come from Gambia, Haiti, Jamaica, Nigeria, or Senegal. People labeled white may have ancestors who come from England, Germany, Ireland, or Italy. In addition, labeling is the result of social definitions more so than it is a result of biological inheritance. For example, in the United States, it was often the case that if one had even one black ancestor then the person would be labeled black regardless of the person's physical appearance.

SOCIAL ISSUE

Has inequality lessened in America? Since the 1960s, have the differences between blacks and whites in education, occupation, and income disappeared?

Equality of opportunity for blacks and whites may be difficult to measure, but comparisons in terms of educational attainment, occupational attainment, and income are objective measures of status that are obtainable from census statistics. Occupation, education, and income are good indicators of social standing. If blacks and whites are becoming more equal in terms of these three criteria, one could say that equality is becoming a reality.

Let's examine these three factors since 1960 and determine the extent of equality. This exercise allows you to compare black and white status attainment to answer the question, Is the status of blacks and whites equal?

ANALYSIS

1. Table 9.1 on page 90 presents data on educational achievement for both white and black Americans. Data on gender is also presented in the table. Based on the data from Table 9.1, complete Tables 9.1A, 9.1B, 9.1C, 9.1D.

2. A. Describe the pattern you see for male high school graduate category.

B. Female high school graduate category.

TABLE 9.1 Percent of Persons Who Are High School Graduates and More, and Bachelor's Degree or More By Race and Sex: 1980 to 1995

| | 1995 | | | | 1980 | | | |
| | Black | | White | | Black | | White | |
	Male	Female	Male	Female	Male	Female	Male	Female
High School Graduate or More	73.4	74.1	83.0	83.0	51.1	51.3	71.0	70.1
Bachelor's Degree or More	13.6	12.9	27.2	21.0	7.7	8.1	22.1	14.0

Source: *Statistical Abstract of the U.S.: 1996*, Table 241, p. 159.

TABLE 9.1A Male High School Graduate or More

	Black	White	Difference
1995			_____
1980			_____

TABLE 9.1B Female High School Graduate or More

	Black	White	Difference
1995			_____
1980			_____

TABLE 9.1C   **Male Bachelor's Degree or More**

	Black	White	Difference
1995			_____
1980			_____

TABLE 9.1D   Female Bachelor's Degree or More

	Black	White	Difference
1995			_____
1980			_____

C. Male bachelor's degree category.

D. Female bachelor's degree category.

3. Evidence of equality or inequality may appear in patterns of earnings. Table 9.2 presents data on median earnings for college graduates by occupational category. The three categories listed in the table are the highest occupational categories listed by the census bureau. One way to analyze this data is to calculate a ratio relating white earnings to black earnings. For example, to compare the earnings of black and white male executives, administrators and managers one would do the following:

$$\frac{\text{Black male earnings}}{\text{White male earnings}} \times 100 \text{ or } \frac{34,858}{48,308} \times 100 = .72$$

The .72 may be interpreted by stating that black male college graduates who are executives, administrators, and managers earn $.72 on the $1.00 as compared to their white counterparts.

Based on the data in Table 9.2 calculate the following ratios.

A. Executives, Administrators, Managers

　　　Black Male/White Male　　　_____

　　　Black Female/White Female　　　_____

B. Professional Specialty Workers

　　　Black Male/White Male　　　_____

　　　Black Female/White Female　　　_____

TABLE 9.2   Median Earnings of Full-Time Workers, 25 Years Old and Over by Occupation, Race, and Sex: 1994

| | Black | | White | |
Occupation	Male	Female	Male	Female
Executive, Administrative & Managerial	34,858	30,939	48,308	31,031
Professional Specialty Workers	36,080	32,208	47,379	32,864
Technical & Related Support Workers	31,324	26,425	37,112	28,376

Source: U.S. Bureau of the Census, unpublished data, May 1996.

C. Technical and Related Support Workers

Black Male/White Male _____

Black Female/White Female _____

4. Describe the general pattern of earnings differences based on your calculations.

5. What factors may contribute to the smaller differentials for females?

6. Another approach one may use to examine differences in income is to examine overall earnings averages. Table 9.3 presents data on median earnings for year round full time workers.

Calculate the difference in median earnings and place your answer in the table.

TABLE 9.3 Median Earnings for Year Round Full Time Workers by Race, and Sex: 1995

	Male	Female
White	33,515	24,264
Black	24,798	21,079
White/Black Difference	_____	_____

Source: *Current Population Reports,* P. 60, No. 193, Sept. 1996.

7. What factors might contribute to the overall difference in earnings?

TABLE 9.4   Persons below Poverty Status by Race: 1979–1994

| | Persons below Poverty Status | | | |
| | White | | Black | |
	Number[1]	Percent	Number	Percent
1979	17,214	9.0	8,050	31.0
1989	20,788	10.0	9,305	30.7
1992	24,523	11.6	10,613	33.3
1994	25,379	11.7	10,196	30.6

Source: *Statistical Abstract of the U.S.: 1996,* Table 730, p. 472.
[1]Number in thousands.

8. Another measure of economic well-being is a comparison of the percentage of persons below poverty level by race. See Table 9.4.

A. For all years shown in Table 9.4, which group has the highest *number*

of persons living below the poverty status? _____

B. For all years shown, which group has the highest *percent* of persons living below the poverty status? _____

C. How much greater is the percentage of blacks living below poverty level than whites for the following years:

1979 _____1989 _____1992 _____1994 _____

9. What factors may have contributed to the increase in the numbers of persons, both black and white, living below poverty status between the years 1979 and 1994?

TABLE 9.5 Percent of Unemployed Workers by Race, and Sex: 1984–1995

Year	White	Black	Difference	White	Black	Difference
		Male			Female	
1995	4.9	10.6	_____	4.8	10.2	_____
1992	6.9	15.2	_____	6.0	13.0	_____
1990	4.8	11.8	_____	4.6	10.8	_____
1988	4.7	11.7	_____	4.7	11.7	_____
1986	6.0	14.6	_____	6.1	14.2	_____
1984	6.4	16.4	_____	6.5	15.4	_____

Source: *Statistical Abstract of the U.S.: 1996,* Table 628, p. 405.

10. Another indicator of occupational status and economic well-being is the percent unemployed by race. Calculate the percent difference by race.

11. Describe the pattern for males derived from your calculations.

12. Describe the pattern for females derived from your calculations.

13. Does equality exist in the United States? Why or why not?

14. What other kinds of research might you undertake to further explore the issue of equality in the United States?

15. Have you ever treated people unfairly because of their background (religion, gender, or ethnic category)? If so, why do you believe you acted in the way you did?

MODULE **10**

CAN YOU AFFORD TO GET SICK?

Health….a blessing money cannot buy.—IZAAK WALTON

The health of the people is really the foundation upon which all their happiness and all their powers as a state depend.
—BENJAMIN DISRAELI

Health care is a major social concern of both Congress and the American public. The government is concerned with the escalating costs of Medicare and Medicaid. Businesses are concerned with the rising costs of health insurance. The average working person worries that if he or she is laid off or changes jobs there will be no health insurance. Those individuals who have no health insurance worry that if a medical emergency arises they will be unable to afford care. There is general agreement that something needs to be done to contain costs and to make sure that every American can get medical treatment. The question is how to accomplish this. Some such as President Clinton advocate a national health care system under the jurisdiction of the government. Others believe that we don't need a new system, but need to fix the current private enterprise system. Those that favor fixing the current system worry that if the government takes over health care the quality of care may decline and that people may lose their ability to choose their own doctors and type of medical treatment. Although there is disagreement as to how to guarantee universal coverage, there is general agreement that U.S. medicine is one of the best in the world.

Most Americans have medical coverage either through private insurance or government programs. Approximately 57 percent have health insurance through their employment. Another 8 percent are privately insured. Government programs such as Medicare (for the elderly), Medicaid (for the poor), and military benefits cover another 20 percent. That means that at any given time, only about 15 percent of the population is without medical coverage. The question becomes how to guarantee these individuals medical coverage.

If you are covered by medical insurance, you may not have given much thought to the cost of health care. After all, you probably figure that you don't need to worry, because if you do get sick your insurance company will pay the bill. Unfortunately, health care costs may be a greater problem than you imagine. In 1960, Americans spent about $27 billion on health care. Today that figure has risen well over $752 billion, which represents an increase of 2,685 percent. The United States spends more on health care than any other nation. For example, the United States spends 50 percent more than Canada and 126 percent more than Japan.

Private funds, which include insurance coverage, cover only about 57 percent of expenses. The other 43 percent comes from public funds, which means that your tax dollars are helping to pay for medical expenses. The cost to you is probably much greater than you realize. If medical costs continue to rise, where will this money come from?

With rising costs, another concern becomes what should be considered essential care? Should coverage include such things as heart transplants, in vitro fertilization, cosmetic surgery? A study published in *The New England Journal of Medicine* estimates that in vitro fertilization (test tube babies) cost the health care system on average $72,000. Currently some insurance policies cover treatment, others don't. Six states require coverage by insurance providers.

Has anyone in your family spent a few days in the hospital recently? If so, you were probably shocked at the cost of medical care. The average cost of one day in the hospital is $931 (1994). Multiply that by the average length of stay of 7 days and you will have some idea of how expensive a typical stay in the hospital is.

The average college student probably isn't worried about having an extended stay in the hospital. In fact, most college students have few health problems, so you may not be too concerned at the moment with the high cost of medical care. Your first experience with it may come when a grandparent has a medical emergency, such as a heart attack. It is not unusual for a person recovering from a heart attack to spend three or more weeks in the hospital. The bill for hospitalization can easily reach $17,220 or more. This figure does not include additional expenses, such as the cost of an operation. The cost of a bypass operation, for example, has been estimated at $39,500 or more.

In all likelihood, the first time that you are faced with the cost of hospital care will not be for an emergency. Rather, it may be when you get married and decide to have a family. To most people, the expected birth of a child is a joyous occasion. Yet very often the parents-to-be are shocked to learn how much it costs to have a baby. In most instances, childbirth does not involve complicated medical procedures. It is regarded as a natural event. However, an uncomplicated pregnancy and delivery can cost $5,000 or more. This figure can increase rapidly if the mother or child needs any special care. Intensive care for a premature baby could run as high as $200,000 or more.

Because medical costs can be so high, most people have some sort of health insurance to protect them from unexpected emergencies as well as to provide them with routine medical care. Insurance coverage, however, varies a great deal. In the past, many people had both hospital and major medical insurance. Hospital insurance covered care and major medical covered doctor's bills. In most instances, major medical insurance covered only expenses connected with illness or injuries and did not cover preventive care. For example, one's annual physical exam or a baby's inoculations were not covered. However, the individual had the right to choose his or her own doctor. Today, as a cost-saving measure, traditional insurance policies are being replaced by memberships in HMOs (health maintenance organizations). HMOs differ from traditional insurance in that HMOs either hire or contract with a large number of doctors for care at a set price. Members of HMOs then pay a yearly fee for health care which includes preventive care. There may be an additional nominal charge of say $10.00 per doctor's visit. There are usually no insurance forms to fill out. The disadvantage is that an individual enrolled in an HMO can only use doctors affiliated with that plan. HMOs, however, have proved to be quite popular. The number of HMOs has grown from 236 plans in 1980 to 550 in 1995. In 1995, there were approximately 46 million people enrolled in HMOs.

The amount and type of health care coverage that the average person has is dependent upon which plans are available either privately or through employers and on what one can afford to pay. Not all plans cover every medical contingency. Most, for example, do not cover nursing home care. Many have a cap on expenditures.

In this exercise you will examine the increasing cost of medical care and determine whether or not that cost has risen faster than the cost of other goods and services. However, the statistics given here cannot explain why the costs have increased. There are a number of contributing factors. Inflation is one of them. Just as the prices of all goods and services have increased over time due to inflation, so too has the cost of health care. A second factor is increasing life expectancy. Because more people are living longer, there are more who become vulnerable to the degenerative ailments of old age: myocardial infarctions (heart attacks), malignant neoplasms (cancer), and cerebral vascular problems (strokes). It is somewhat ironic that one of the greatest dreams of humankind is to be able to extend life expectancy, yet along with the achievement of that dream comes a wide range of related problems. If more people are living longer, then more people are vulnerable to a wider range of illnesses. There is a strain on the health care industry because more people are living long enough to have need of it.

A third factor is the high cost of medical research and technology. A magnetic resonance imaging scanner (MRI) can cost from $1 to $2 million dollars. In 1990 it is estimated that more than 5 million MRI scans were performed at a cost of $5 billion dollars.[1] Medical researchers are constantly developing new ways in which to treat illness. Dialysis machines and artificial hearts are examples of devices based on new technology. Other research is aimed at finding cures for diseases such as cancer and AIDS. New types of drugs, new surgical techniques, and new types of medical technology add dramatically to the cost of health care.

Although a great boon to health care, these innovations are very costly. It takes a great deal of time and effort to develop them, and the research process is very expensive. Once discovered, new drugs and machinery can be very costly to produce. In the end, the consumer must pay for all the expenses involved.

In addition to the problem of its high cost, there are other issues associated with health care. An analysis of cost data does not treat the quality of health care. It is getting more expensive, but is it getting better? The evidence here is mixed. In some instances terminally ill patients who are brain dead or in a comatose condition with no chance of recovery are kept alive through the use of life support systems. Should the life support equipment be turned off? This type of question, which poses a moral dilemma, is becoming more prevalent.

On the one hand, there is greater availability of health care today than in the past and there are improved methods of treatment. Some patients who in the past would have died now recover fully. With increased knowledge, quality in some areas is vastly improved, For example, it is only in the relatively recent past that hospitals have set up special units for emergency heart ailments. These are often called Coronary Care Units (C.C.U.). Victims of heart attacks are separated from other patients and given special care. These patients are constantly monitored, and these units are staffed by specially trained nurses. It is highly probable that thousands of lives have been saved because of the existence of such units.

On the other hand, some medical practices have come under public scrutiny and have been severely criticized. One example is the widespread use of caesarean sections. In recent years the number of births by Caesarean section has risen substantially. Medical practitioners argue that this is due to greater awareness of the problems associated with the birth process, and that many infants have been saved or prevented from being brain damaged by this technique. Some doctors believe that Caesarean births have become commonplace because of the risk of a malpractice suit and therefore, doctors perform caesareans to protect themselves. Some critics have suggested that physicians prefer caesareans, so they can schedule the time of birth at their convenience. In addition, doctors generally charge a higher fee for Caesarean sections than they do for natural births.

Certainly there is evidence to suggest that doctors and hospitals often engage in excessive medical testing on patients. This may partly be due to the fact that doctors and hospitals are concerned with protecting themselves from the risk of malpractice suits from the increasingly litigious U.S. public.

Related to the problem of quality of health care is the problem of its distribution. There is a wide range of differences in the availability of health care, depending on where you live. Some people may live over 100 miles from a major hospital, while others live two blocks away from a university medical center. The number of available doctors is also unequally distributed. In large urban areas there tends to be a greater availability of qualified physicians than in rural areas. Even within a given urban area there may be wide variations. In poorer sections, medical care often consists of publicly supported clinics, which are usually understaffed and the doctors are often overworked. In wealthier sections, the number of physicians and specialists is apt to be much higher. Physicians, like other occupational groups, tend to flock to areas where the earning potential is greatest.

SOCIAL ISSUE

Can you afford to get sick? Many people, today, are concerned with the high cost of medical care and worry about their ability to pay for a medical emergency. What if they found out they had cancer, or that they needed a coronary bypass? Could they afford the cost of treatment?

The cost of medical care has risen over the years, and there is concern that the costs will continue to rise. How have the costs of medical care risen in terms of other expenditures? Do medical expenditures represent a larger proportion of the consumer price index (CPI) than in the past?

In order to analyze shifts in medical expenses, you need to examine the average cost of medical care by year. Various types of medical costs can be compared by year: the average cost of a doctor's office visit, the cost of particular operations, or the cost of a day in the hospital. In this exercise, you will examine some of these costs. After completing this exercise you may want to go to the library and look up other types of medical expenses, such as the cost of a heart transplant, the cost of treatment for an AIDS patient, or the cost of malpractice insurance for different medical specialities.

ANALYSIS

1. Let's examine Table 10.1, which gives the average cost of a day in the hospital, and the average cost per stay for 1975, 1980, 1985, 1990, 1993, and 1994. Immediately, you can see that the costs have increased dramatically from 1975 to 1994. Compute the percentage increase in the costs from 1975 to 1994. Remember the formula for finding a percent change is:

$$\frac{T_2 - T_1}{T_1} \text{ or } \frac{1994 \text{ amount} - 1975 \text{ amount}}{1975 \text{ amount}} \times 100 = \text{percent change}$$

A plus answer would represent the percent increase and a minus answer the percent decrease.

TABLE 10.1 Average Hospital Costs 1975–1994

Type		Average Cost per Day	Average Cost per Stay
Year	1975	$134	$1,030
	1980	$245	$1,851
	1985	$460	$3,245
	1990	$687	$4,947
	1993	$881	$6,132
	1994	$931	$6,230

Source: *Statistical Abstract of the United States: 1996*, Table 190, p.129;
Statistical Abstract of the United States: 1985, Table 186, p. 127.

Now compute the percentage change for each.

Type of expenditure   Percent change 1975–1994

Cost per day   _____

Cost per stay   _____

2. What are some factors that might help to account for the increase in hospital care costs?

3. Using the data given in Tables 10.1 and 10.2, compute the average cost for hospitalization for the following diseases or procedures in 1985 and 1993.

TABLE 10.2 Average Stay in Hospital and Average Cost by Type of Disease or Procedure: 1985–1993

Type of Disease or Procedure	Average Number of Days in Hospital	Average Cost per Stay	Average Number of Days in Hospital	Average Cost per Stay
	1985		1993	
Heart disease	7.0	_____	6.0	_____
Malignant neoplasm	9.1	_____	8.5	_____
Fracture	7.7	_____	6.7	_____
Childbirth	3.3	_____	2.4	_____

Source: *Statistical Abstract of the United States: 1996,* Table 196, p. 132; *Statistical Abstract of the United States: 1988,* Table 160, p. 101.

4. For each of the diseases or procedures in Table 10.2, what other types of medical expenses would you have? Discuss them.

5. As you can see from your calculations in Table 10.2, even though the average number of days of hospitalization for each disease or procedure decreased, the cost of the average stay increased. Calculate the percent change in the cost of the average stay for each procedure or disease from 1985 to 1993.

1985–1993
Percent Change in Average
Cost Per Hospital Stay

Heart disease   _____

Malignant neoplasm   _____

Fracture   _____

Childbirth   _____

6. The costs you have computed indicate the high cost of medical care, but how do these costs compare to other consumer expenditures? Now let's examine the average annual percent change in the consumer price index and compare it to the average annual percent change in medical care expenses. This will give you some idea of whether or not medical expenses have increased more rapidly than other types of consumer expenditures. It also takes into account the effect of inflation. For Table 10.3 compute the percent difference between the CPI and the cost of medical care.

TABLE 10.3   Average Annual Percent Difference in Consumer Price Index and Cost of Medical Care from 1960–1995

Years	Percent Change in CPI	Average Percent Change in Cost of Medical Care	Percent Difference
1960–1965	1.3	2.5	_____
1965–1970	4.3	6.2	_____
1970–1975	6.8	6.9	_____
1975–1980	8.9	9.5	_____
1980–1985	5.5	8.7	_____
1985–1990	4.0	7.5	_____
1990–1995	3.0	5.8	_____

Source: *Health: United States: 1995*, Table 117, p. 242.

7. In what time period was there the largest percent difference in the two

indexes? _____

8. In any year was the percent change in medical costs less than the percent

change in the consumer price index? _____

9. Looking at Table 10.3, which set of figures, medical costs or the CPI, has

been increasing at a faster rate? _____

10. What are some of the variables or factors that might account for the pattern you see in Table 10.3? Discuss.

11. There are many components to medical care costs, but three important ones are doctors' fees, hospital rooms, and prescription drugs. Let's examine the percentage increases in costs for each of these three to determine if the costs of the three have increased equally. Examine Table 10.4.

TABLE 10.4   **Average Annual Percent Change for Medical Care Components of Consumer Price Index from 1975–1995**

Medical Care	Physician's Costs	Hospital Room	Prescription Drugs
1975–1980	9.7	12.2	7.2
1980–1985	8.2	11.2	10.6
1985–1990	7.3	8.7	8.6
1990–1995	5.2	7.0	4.5

Source: *Health: United States: 1995,* Table 117, p. 242.

a. Which component rose the fastest in 1975–1980? _____

b. Which component rose the fastest in 1980–1985? _____

c. Which component rose the fastest in 1985–1990? _____

c. Which component rose the fastest in 1990–1995? _____

12. What variables or factors might account for the increase in physician's fees?

13. What factors might account for the increase in hospital room fees?

14. What factors might account for the increase in the cost of prescription drugs?

15. How do people pay for these rising costs? Table 10.5 presents data on sources of funds.

Where does the money come from to pay for medical costs? There are two major sources: private and public. Private sources include personal outlays by consumers, insurance companies, and charitable organizations. Public sources include payments by federal, state, and local governments. From 1975 to 1994, what has been the percent increase in all health expenses?

***

TABLE 10.5 **National Health Care Expenditures According to Source of Funds: U.S. Selected Years 1975–1994**

Year	All Health Expenses in Billions	Private Funds Amount per Capita	Percent of Total	Public Funds Amount per Capita	Percent of Total
1975	$130.7	$337	57.9	$245	42.1
1980	$247.2	$606	57.6	$446	42.4
1985	$428.2	$1,029	59.3	$706	40.7
1990	$697.5	$1,592	59.2	$1,096	40.8
1994	$949.4	$1,954	55.7	$1,556	44.3

Source: *Health: United States: 1995,* Table 118, p. 243.

16. What has been the percent increase from 1975 to 1994 in per capita expenditures?

a. From private sources _____

b. From public sources _____

17. In the United States, expenditures for health care account for a larger proportion of the gross domestic product (GDP) than for any other country. GDP is the total market value of goods and services. The increase in the amount spent on health care has been seen by some as rather alarming and as pointing to the need for reform. Examine Table 10.6 and calculate what percent more the United States spends than each of the other ten countries.

TABLE 10.6   Total Health Expenditures as Percent of Gross Domestic Product: Selected Countries, 1993[1]

Country	Percent	Percent More Spent by U.S.
Australia	8.5	_____
Canada	10.2	_____
France	9.8	_____
Germany	8.6	_____
Greece	5.7	_____
Ireland	6.7	_____
Italy	8.5	_____
Japan	7.3	_____
Sweden	7.5	_____
United Kingdom	7.1	_____
United States	13.6	_____

Source: *Statistical Abstract for the United States: 1995*, Table 115, p. 240.
[1]Preliminary figures.

TABLE 10.7 Gross Domestic Product and National Health Expenditures: United States 1960–1994

Year	Percent Gross Domestic Product	Amount Per Capita
1960	5.1	$141
1970	7.1	$341
1980	8.9	$1,052
1990	12.1	$2,688
1994	13.7	$3,510

Source: *Health: United States: 1995,* Table 114, p. 239.

18. United States spending on health care has increased dramatically since 1960. The increase in spending has been seen by some as alarming and pointing to the need to reform. Examine Table 10.7.

a. Calculate the percent increase in the percent of GDP spent on health care from 1960 to 1994. _____

b. Calculate the percent increase in the amount per capita spent on health care from 1960 to 1994. _____

19. Health care costs have risen substantially over the years. What policies do you believe can be developed to alleviate this problem?

20. If someone in your family were to get very ill today, how would you and your family pay for the expenses? What difficulties do you believe you would encounter in meeting these financial obligations?

ENDNOTES

1. Public Health Agenda, *The Health Care Crisis,* NY: McGraw-Hill, 1992, p. 13.

MODULE **11**

AIDS: THE MODERN PLAGUE?

*The emotional well-being of people with AIDS is undermined
by physical disease, weakness, and pain, by the likely immi-
nence of death, and by stigmatization, social oppression, and
pervasive loss.*
—U.S. DEPARTMENT OF HEALTH
AND HUMAN SERVICES, 1986

In the fourteenth and fifteenth centuries, Europe was ravaged by the Black
Death. The bubonic plague was carried by fleas on the backs of rats. The tiny
but virulent bacillus carried by the fleas caused the deaths of close to two-
thirds of Europe's population. This disease caused terror all over Europe and in
many ways altered the course of history in that part of the world.

Although no one equates AIDS with the bubonic plague, many people are
very much concerned with both the short-term and long-term impact AIDS
may have on the United States and on other parts of the world. By 1996 362,000
Americans have died of AIDS. It is also estimated that between one and one-half
million Americans may be infected with the virus that causes AIDS. In this module, you will analyze some of the most recent data on AIDS. Specifically, you
will review where AIDS cases occur and who are the most likely victims of the
disease. From this data, you will be asked to discern patterns of the disease and
ultimately attempt to put the problem of AIDS into perspective. Prior to analyzing the problem let us examine some basic information regarding the disease.

No one is certain how or where the disease began. Some experts suggest
that the virus that contributes to the development of AIDS may be very old. In
its original state it may have been harmless to humans. Then, some thirty
years ago, and this is only a rough estimate, the virus underwent some form
of mutation, a sudden change in its genetic makeup. This mutation made the
virus life-threatening to humans. Probably starting in Central Africa, the disease quickly spread to other continents. Cases of AIDS have now been reported
in a number of countries as varied and as distant from each other as Malawi,
Burundi, Italy, Switzerland, Germany, Haiti, and of course the United States.

The United Nations estimates that between ten and twelve million persons worldwide have been infected with HIV. What is even more alarming are some of the projections now being made by researchers. The United Nations suggests that by the year 2000 there will be between 30 and 40 million cases of AIDS with an even larger number of persons carrying the virus. These large numbers become even more dramatic when one takes into the account the possibility, as suggested by some, that the number of cases in the industrialized nations is leveling off. The bulk of new cases will come from the developing nations of the world. Several nations in sub-Saharan Africa have had alarmingly dramatic increases in the number of AIDS cases. Even though Africa accounts for only 10 percent of the world's population, according to the best estimates, it has two-thirds of the world's AIDS cases.

There is no clear consensus as to the nature of the disease. There is much ongoing research as to the causes and the dynamics of the illness. Following is a brief summary of what is known about AIDS. The virus that causes AIDS is called the HIV infection or the Human Immuno-deficiency Virus. Again, there is no total agreement on the nature of this virus. One of the factors that contributes to the problem of analyzing the disease is that AIDS is probably due to the HIV virus and a number of cofactors. Among the cofactors that may be significant in developing AIDS are the individual's general health, diet, and the presence of other types of infections. A recent presidential report urged that greater focus be given to the HIV infection. It is this infection that may lead to ARC (AIDS-related complex) and to the disease commonly referred to as AIDS.

If the HIV infection is present, the individual becomes vulnerable to a variety of illnesses. The virus attacks the individual's immune system by attacking the white blood cells—the lymphocytes. This is how the term AIDS is derived—Acquired Immune Deficiency Syndrome. When the immunological system is weakened, the body becomes a target for what are termed *opportunistic infections*. These infections are not usually life threatening because most individuals' immune systems can defend the body against such infections. However, if the immunological system becomes damaged due to the invasion of the HIV infection, then an individual becomes susceptible to the illnesses. To be more specific, two illnesses quite common among AIDS patients are Pneumocystic Carinii Pneumonia and Kaposi's Sarcoma, a type of cancer. Individuals would not be susceptible to either one of these illnesses unless they contacted the HIV infection.

How is this disease transmitted? From a sociological perspective, this is one of the most interesting areas to discuss. A mythology about the causes and spread of the disease of AIDS has developed. One often hears people talking about how one should be careful using toilet seats in public bathrooms; or, one should be concerned with whom they kiss; or, even the belief that there may be danger of contacting AIDS through something as common as shaking hands. None of these notions is supported by scientific evidence. The transmission of this disease occurs through the exchange of specific bodily fluids: semen and blood. There are some reports that the disease may also be transmitted through vaginal secretions and breast milk but there is no conclusive evidence to support this contention. There is agreement, however, that the virus can be transmitted by having sexual contact with an infected person; by receiving blood in a transfusion from a donor whose blood has been contaminated by the virus; by an unborn child receiving the virus through the placenta from his or her infected mother; and by an intravenous (IV) drug user from a syringe that has been used by someone infected with the virus.

Unfortunately, there is still much we do not know about this disease. For example, it is not known why the disease may spread more rapidly in some areas than in other areas, or why some infected people survive for much longer periods of time than others. Scientists have yet to understand why the body's immune system has been ineffective in protecting infected persons. AIDS may consist of a number of different viral strains. Medical practitioners have yet to come up with the exact number of strains that exist.

While medical research has yet to develop a cure or preventative measures for the disease, some recent research has had promising results. Researchers are currently utilizing various combinations of drugs to treat AIDS patients. These families of drugs do not constitute a cure; however, they do appear to prolong the lives of some of the persons who have been infected.

Why is there such ignorance concerning this particular disease? There are three factors contributing to the general lack of knowledge and misunderstanding by the public. First, the disease itself is very new. It first received official recognition by the U.S. Centers for Disease Control in 1981. Second, the transmission of this disease involves human sexual behavior. Traditionally, Americans have been somewhat reticent to openly discuss anything having to do with human sexuality. Therefore, the sexual nature of the transmission process deters open and honest discussion. The third factor is related to the one just mentioned. This illness has become most prevalent among homosexuals and drug users. Homosexuality for a long period of time has been a subject not open to public discussion or concern. The public at large may take the view that AIDS is *their* problem. This same perception relates to the IV drug users. Drug addicts, it is believed, belong to someone else's family and therefore it is not a concern for most Americans.

Many experts suggest that it is within the heterosexual community that the HIV infection will have its greatest increase. As this information becomes better known, Americans will become more concerned with the problem as it will affect them more directly.

This module is designed to make you more knowledgeable about the problem of AIDS. You will be given the opportunity to analyze some current data on the illness. As an end result of this analysis, it is hoped that you will be more aware of the problem and gain greater insights into its nature.

SOCIAL ISSUE

How serious is the problem of AIDS? Are we facing a new plague in our society? This module will give you the opportunity to gain a better understanding of this important problem.

ANALYSIS

1. Before we look at the problem of AIDS in the United States, let us briefly examine it from an international perspective. Table 11.1 presents data on the number of reported AIDS cases by world region. Calculate the percentage distribution of the disease on a worldwide basis.

TABLE 11.1   Estimated Distribution of HIV-infected Adults Alive as of Mid-1995

Region	Number of Cases	Percent
Africa and Middle East	9,000,000	_____
Americas	2,250,000	_____
Asia	3,050,000	_____
Europe and Central Asia	500,000	_____
Australia	20,000	_____
Total	14,820,000	_____

Source: The National AIDS Strategy, 1997.

2. In a few sentences, describe the distribution of AIDS cases on a worldwide basis.

TABLE 11.2   AIDS Reported by Leading Metropolitan Areas with 500,000 or More Population: 1996

Metropolitan Area	Number	Rate[1]
San Francisco	1,572	95.0
New York	10,385	120.1
Los Angeles	3,715	40.7
Washington, D.C.	2,160	47.3
Chicago	1,841	23.8

Source: *HIV/AIDS Surveillance Report*, U.S. Department of Health and Human Services, Dec. 1996.
[1]Rate per 100,000 population.

3. As you can see, AIDS cases are not evenly distributed around the world. The same is true for cases within the United States. Examine Table 11.2, and answer the following questions.

a. Which metropolitan area has the largest number of cases?

_____

b. Why do you think this area has the largest number of cases?

c. Which metropolitan area has the largest rate of cases?

_____

d. Why do you think this area has the largest rate?

4. Why do you think these five metropolitan areas are in the top five for reported cases of AIDS?

TABLE 11.3   Reported AIDS Cases by Year

Year	Number of Reported Cases
1987	21,478 ·
1990	41,639
1996	66,816

Source: *Statistical Abstract of the United States: 1996,* Table 217, p. 142.
HIV/AIDS Surveillance Report, Dec. 1996.

> **5.** Now, let us see how rapidly the number of reported cases of AIDS is increasing. Look at Table 11.3. How would you describe the changes you observe in Table 11.3?

> **6.** Who is most likely to get AIDS? Table 11.4 presents data on the lifestyles of those who have developed the disease. In order to get a clearer picture of who are the victims, calculate the percent distribution for each lifestyle category.

TABLE 11.4   Reported Cases of AIDS by Transmission Category for Adults/ Adolescent Cases Reported through December 1996

Transmission Category	Number of Cases	Percent
Men who have sex with men	287,576	_____
Injecting drug use	146,359	_____
Men who have sex with men and injecting drug use	37,152	_____
Hemophilia/coagulation disorder	4,443	_____
Heterosexual contact	49,764	_____
Receipt of blood transfusion, blood components, or tissue	7,888	_____
Other/risk not identified	40,618	_____
Total	573,800	_____

Source: *HIV/AIDS Surveillance Report*, U.S. Department of Health and Human Services, Dec. 1996.

7. Which group has the highest percentage of victims? _____

8. Which group has the second highest percentage? _____

9. What percentage of victims are from these two groups combined?

_____

10. Why are these groups dominant in the victim categories?

11. As you can see, the homosexual and drug abuser lifestyles are most susceptible to this disease. Why then is there a growing concern in the general society about the threat of AIDS?

12. At the time this module was written a great deal of research was being done in the area of AIDS. Assuming no medical treatment or cure has been found since this book was published, what social policies might we develop to try to curtail the spread of the HIV infection that leads to AIDS?

13. What would you do if a close friend told you he or she has the HIV infection?

MODULE **12**

ARE WE DESTROYING OUR ENVIRONMENT?

We shall never understand the natural environment until we see it as a living organism. Land can be healthy or sick, fertile, or barren, rich or poor, lovingly nurtured or bled white. Our present attitudes and laws governing the ownership and use of land represent an abuse of the concept of private property…In America today you can murder land for private profit, You can leave the corpse for all to see, and nobody calls the cops.
—PAUL BROOKS

On Saturday, 26 April 1986, an accident occurred in a small city in what was then called the Soviet Union. The city was Chernobyl, and the accident occurred in a nuclear power plant. Almost 3 million people lived within 150 miles of that nuclear power plant. Their health was certainly endangered by the accident. Perhaps even more dramatically, millions of people living outside the Soviet Union, in Poland, Yugoslavia, Austria, Sweden, and elsewhere, were greatly alarmed by the accident. Air quality, the underground water system, agricultural products, livestock, and ultimately, people will all be affected by the accident at Chernobyl. It may take years to realize the long-term effects of this accident. Non-nuclear pollution can also have a dramatic effect on the environment. For example, on 2 August 1990, Iraqi troops entered the emirate of Kuwait. Within six months the United States led an allied force against Iraqi troops with the goal of removing them from Kuwait. One year after the initial incursion by Iraq's soldiers there were still over 500 oil wells on fire in Kuwait. These fires were sending smoke plumes some 12,000 feet into the air. In addition to creating extensive air pollution, the conflict also contributed to water pollution and threatened at least four species of fish and animals. The short-term effects of this pollution have been devastating. The long-term effects of this pollution remain to be seen.

There are few issues that have as direct an effect on you as does the issue of environmental pollution. Environmental pollution may have a direct impact on your health, on the health of your family, friends, and neighbors, and for those of you who plan to have children, on the health of your as yet unborn infants. The food you eat, the water you drink, and the air you breathe are all affected by environmental pollution.

In order to gain an understanding of the problem of pollution we need to have an understanding of the relationship of people to the environment. Unlike other species, human beings do not passively accept the environment as they find it. Humans are innovators, creators, and active participants in the environment. To some degree, all species interact with their environment. But no species makes such an impact on the environment as do humans. For example, we can take a vast wilderness and convert it into an artificial environment called a city. We can take a river and redirect its waters through the use of dams. Humans take the natural environment and use it for their own purposes to a degree unmatched in nature.

Today we are in the midst of an ongoing debate concerning the relationship of humans to the environment. On one side are environmentalists, people who are concerned with preserving the environment in its natural state. They view the environment as a national treasure to be preserved for future generations. Their major concern is that if humans interfere with the delicate balance in nature, devastating effects may result, such as the elimination of a number of species of plants and animals, irreversible air and water pollution, and the destruction of vast recreational areas.

In opposition to this view are a variety of business and labor organizations. They view the environment as a resource to be used by humans for development. Specifically, many business and labor leaders are concerned with economic growth and expansion and want to use the natural environment to help create jobs, build profits, and expand economic resources.

Underlying this debate is a conflict in basic values. It is important that the society as a whole decide upon what its policy will be vis-a-vis the environment. However, in a pluralistic society such as the United States, where there are a number of different groups representing their own values and interests, it is very difficult to arrive at a consensus.

A number of different topics may be listed under the heading of environmental pollution. Radioactive nuclear waste materials, carbon monoxide and lead from truck and automobile exhaust systems, toxic chemicals dumped illegally, oil spills from tankers, noise pollution, and cigarette smoke may all be considered part of the environmental pollution problem. And this is by no means an exhaustive list. For example, during the summer of 1988 a number of beaches in the New York City area had to be closed because used medical wastes (i.e., syringes) washed ashore. In all likelihood, this pollution was a result of illegal dumping of hospital waste materials.

Another illustration of the extent of pollution is the number of days a year a given area is said to have poor air quality standards. In 1994, the Los Angeles-

Anaheim-Riverside area in California exceeded the limits for 88 days. That is almost one-fourth of the year.

Because of our concern with hazardous waste contamination, the federal government is in the process of establishing over 1,200 hazardous waste dump sites throughout the United States. New Jersey will have 107 of these sites; Pennsylvania will have 103 sites, followed closely by California with 96 active or planned sites.

The exercises in this module will focus on three types of pollution: air pollution, water pollution, and the threat of radioactive pollution from nuclear power plants.

Air pollution has been one of the more publicized types of pollution. The problem of air quality in our major urban areas such as New York City and Los Angeles is usually reported every summer. During the so-called dog days of summer we often hear warnings from environmental agencies that the elderly and the sick should remain indoors. Health experts alert us to the dangers of too much exercise when the air quality is poor. A number of citizens have to curtail their activities because of air pollution. The major contributor to this problem is our modern system of transportation. Our cars, trucks, and buses produce many of the harmful components that contribute to the pollution of our air. Recently we have been making efforts to reduce these negative elements—such as using lead-free gasoline.

Water pollution has also received lots of publicity in recent years. A somewhat astonishing indictment came out of a United Nations report in the early 1970s that stated that no major waterway in the world was free of pollution. Since the 1970s there is evidence that the situation has worsened. Water pollution may have a number of effects on us; the most important being that there may be a shortage of water for human consumption. Pollution also makes an impact on the world's fishing industry and a nutritional impact on consumers. Water pollution may affect recreational activities. Water sports including swimming may be halted if our favorite lakes or seashore vacation spots are closed due to pollution. Pollution can also affect the natural balance in the ecosystem of our oceans, rivers, and lakes. Animal and plant life may be affected as well.

The last type of pollution we will discuss is pollution from radioactive wastes. As noted at the beginning of this module, this may be the most dramatic and potentially the most devastating type of pollution. There have been a number of leaks from nuclear power plants, Three Mile Island in Pennsylvania being the most notable example in the United States. Of greater concern is an actual accident, such as the one at Chernobyl, where a substantial amount of radioactive material was released into the atmosphere.

Such an accident has both short- and long-term effects. In the short term, those individuals very close to the accident may die from radioactive poisoning. Local livestock and agricultural products may become contaminated. Underground water systems may be polluted. In the long run, increased rates of miscarriages, babies with birth defects, and increased rates of cancer can be expected in the surrounding area.

All these types of pollution have a direct and dramatic impact on our lives. Let us look at some of the patterns and trends related to environmental pollution in the United States. Are we in fact destroying our planet or are we making an effort to change our behavior to insure the planet's survival?

SOCIAL ISSUE

Are we destroying our environment? What have been the recent patterns with respect to environmental pollution? This module will help you analyze recent trends in this area.

ANALYSIS

Let us examine some national data on pollution to see if there have been any changes in the amount of pollution. First let us look at air pollution. Table 12.1 presents data on two major sources of air pollution: carbon monoxide and lead.

1. Between 1980 and 1994 have air pollution emissions increased or decreased?

_____

2. What has been the percentage change between 1980 and 1994 for carbon monoxide? _____ for lead? _____

TABLE 12.1   National Air Pollution Emissions: 1980-1994

Pollutants	Year	
	1980	1994
Carbon monoxide[1]	115.6	98.0
Lead[2]	75.0	5.0

Source: *Statistical Abstract of the United States: 1996*, Table 374, p. 234.

[1]In millions of metric tons.

[2]In thousands of metric tons.

3. Transport vehicles are the major contributors to the amount of carbon monoxide and lead in the air. This being the case, what factors do you believe contributed to the decline in pollution emissions?

4. Now let us examine some data on water pollution. Examine Table 12.2, which presents data on polluting discharges in American waters.

Calculate the percentage change in incidents and in gallons of polluted materials discharged.

	Incidents	*Gallons*
1975 to 1993	_____	_____

5. What pattern do you find for the time period covered?

TABLE 12.2   Polluting Discharge Reported in and around U.S. Waters: 1975–1993

Year	Incidents	Gallons (1,000)
1975	10,998	21,528
1993	9,672	1,544

Source: *Statistical Abstract of the United States: 1996*, Table 372, p. 233.

6. What factors might contribute to the pattern you found?

7. Pollution is costly. Table 12.3 presents data on overall expenditures related to pollution.

In order to get a clearer picture of the change in expenditures, calculate the percent change for the years:

1980 to 1990 _____

1990 to 1993 _____

1980 to 1993 _____

8. While additional funds may help to cope with the problem of environmental pollution, money is not the only answer. What else might the society as a whole and we as individuals do to curb pollution?

TABLE 12.3 Pollution Abatement and Control Expenditures: 1980–1993

Year	Total Expenditures (Millions)
1980	50,399
1990	93,877
1993	109,044

Source: *Statistical Abstract of the United States: 1996*, Table 384, p. 239.

TABLE 12.4   **Nuclear Power Plants in the U.S.: 1970–1995**

Year	Number of Operable Reactors	Percent Change
1970	18	
1980	70	_____
1990	111	_____
1995	109	_____

Source: *Statistical Abstract of the United States: 1996*, Table 944, p. 593.

9. We introduced this module with a discussion of the nuclear accident at Chernobyl. What about the potential for a nuclear accident in the United States? Table 12.4 presents data on the number of nuclear power reactors in the United States. Calculate the percent change in the number of nuclear power reactors.

10. What do you believe is the reason there had been an increase in the number of reactors?

11. What impact do different value positions have on the development of policies regarding nuclear power? (Hint: Reread the introduction.)

12. Table 12.5 presents data on solid waste generated by people on a day-to-day basis. What is the percent change in the total amount of waste generated from 1970 to 1994? _____

TABLE 12.5 Municipal Solid Waste Generated per Person per Day: 1970–1994

Year	Gross Waste Generated (millions of tons)	Pounds Per Person
1970	121.9	3.3
1980	151.5	3.7
1990	198.0	4.3
1994	209.1	4.4

Source: *Statistical Abstract of the United States: 1996*, Table 380, p. 237.

13. What is the percent change in pounds per person of waste generated

from 1970 to 1994? _____

14. What are some factors that may account for the changes you found in the data?

15. Do you believe we are destroying our environment? Explain.

16. In your day-to-day activities, have you contributed to the problem of pollution? If so, describe the ways in which you have done so.

MODULE **13**

ARE ALL MARRIAGES DOOMED TO FAIL?

Divorce: The past tense of marriage—ANONYMOUS

Not long ago divorce was seen as a disaster. It was an issue that was whispered about; not to be spoken about in front of the children. If someone in the family was going through a divorce, it brought shame and embarrassment to the entire family. The divorced person became the skeleton in the closet. The event became the family secret, not to be discussed with outsiders.

Today, much of the stigma of divorce is gone. Many public schools offer support groups for children of divorced couples. The number of people who are divorced has increased substantially. In 1970 some four million Americans were divorced. In 1995 the figure was approximately seventeen million.

Why has this happened? What has contributed to the two hundred and eighty-one percent increase in the number of persons who have been divorced? One factor has already been noted. With more divorced individuals, the stigma has lessened. This is not to say that divorce is completely accepted. A lifelong marriage is still the ideal. However, it has become more acceptable for people to terminate their marriage if they find themselves in unhappy relationships.

Another factor that contributes to the increase in divorce is a more lenient legal system. In the past, it was extremely difficult to get a divorce. Today, in most states, the legal process for obtaining a divorce has been made easier. The reader should note that this does not mean that a legal divorce is easy to obtain. It may still be a very difficult process involving a long period of time, a great deal of expense, and the emotional turmoil associated with divorce itself. However, as a relatively easier process, it is thus more likely that larger numbers of people would be willing to go through the process. It is possible that in the past there were just as many unhappily married people as there are today. Because of the complexity of the legal system, and because of the stigma attached to divorce, many people may have decided to "stick it out." It is also possible that in the past large numbers of people may have opted for an informal divorce. They may have decided to separate without getting an official divorce.

Another factor that may have contributed to the higher rate of divorce is related to the notion that the family is no longer the all encompassing institution that it once was. It was not that long ago when family members were much more entwined with their family. In the past, the family institution was the center of all of one's activities. Family members worked together, ate together, played together, and prayed together. The family was the central focus for all of one's life. Today, much of this has changed. In the morning, we wake up, the children are sent off to school, the father goes to work in one direction, and the mother goes to work in another direction. The family members may be reunited in the evening, or they may not. One parent may have to work late. A child may have an after school activity, or have plans with one of their friends. The actual physical time spent with family members is a small part of our waking hours.

While in the past there were a number of linkages between family members, today the linkages are fewer. This may be translated by saying that the reasons for staying together are fewer today than in the past. The family unit, and with it marriage, is no longer anchored to a variety of factors. One should be careful not to overstate the case. Individuals still maintain a sense of family. Family members still have a special sense of connection to other family members. But, in terms of everyday activities, the intimate association of family members on a day in, day out basis has, for most families, disappeared. In turn, and not surprisingly, marital relationships are no longer cemented by many of the essential and necessary functions of life. Today, we fulfill these necessary functions as individuals, not as members of family units. For example, work was a family activity. All family members participated in the planting and harvesting of crops. In the urban-industrial society we live in, work is an individual enterprise. Work has become an individual activity. Therefore, reasons to stay together in an unhappy marriage are not as compelling as they once were.

Related to this notion of reduced linkages is a fourth contributing factor. There is little question that the role of women in U.S. society has undergone substantial change in this century. Women are more likely to graduate from high school, graduate from college, and move on to a career. More and more women are entering the professional ranks of the workforce. While unmarried women have always worked, today we see dramatic increases in the number of married women, and women with young children who are also following lifelong patterns of work. For example, over fifty percent of women with children under the age of one re-enter the workforce. This work pattern gives women greater economic independence, and, with it, greater emotional independence. This may lead women to be less accepting of an unhappy marriage.

In addition to the workforce activity, another major change regarding women has been the perception of what it means to be a woman. In the past a woman's identity was intimately tied to the identity of her husband. In a real sense a woman did not have an identity without being married. Today, as more women achieve a higher education, and develop their own career paths, the obligatory ties to their husbands diminish in importance. Divorce would no longer leave a woman without an identity or without a source of income. To some degree, one may say that there are more divorces today because more women can afford to get a divorce.

A last factor that may lead people to be more likely to seek a divorce is related to the impact of divorce on children. In the past, a number of parents may have felt that they had to stay in an unhappy marriage for "the sake of the children." Today, it is felt that an emotionally disruptive household, caused by two parents who are constantly at odds with one another, may be more detrimental to children than divorce. Therefore, divorce may be the lesser of two evils.

In addition to these general sociological factors that contribute to divorce, there are personal factors that may be briefly mentioned. For example, the younger the age at which people marry the greater the chance for divorce. This is especially true if one of the persons marrying is eighteen years of age or younger. It should be somewhat obvious that this has to do with the level of one's maturity, and the person's ability to make sound decisions that are supposed to last them a lifetime.

A second factor is the length of time the couple has known each other prior to getting married. The shorter the period of acquaintanceship, the greater the chance for divorce. Again the explanation should be somewhat obvious. The less time you know the other party, the less you know about them. In theory marriage is a lifelong contract. Therefore, it requires some period of time to get to know the other person.

A third influencing factor is the dissimilarity of backgrounds. This would include such variables as differences in educational attainment, social class, religion, and race. It would also include differences in values, attitudes, and life goals. While opposites may or may not attract, they usually do not make for long lasting marriages.

All of the factors noted above have contributed to the increase in divorce. It should be noted that while divorce has risen since the end of World War II, today divorce rates appear to have leveled off. The rapid increases in the number and rate of divorces that were seen during the late 1960s and early 1970s are no longer occurring. It must be remembered however that the level at which divorce now occurs is still much higher than it was in the past.

SOCIAL ISSUE

Are all marriages doomed to fail? How extensive is divorce? What impact does divorce have on the living arrangements of children? What is its economic impact on children? The analysis section will now give you the opportunity to explore these issues.

ANALYSIS

TABLE 13.1   Marital Status of Total Persons 18 Years Old and Over: 1970–1996

	1996[2]		1980		1970	
	Number (1000)	Percent	Number (1000)	Percent	Number (1000)	Percent
Married	116,562	_____	104,564	_____	94,999	_____
Divorced	18,288	_____	9,886	_____	4,282	_____
Other[1]	69,775	_____	45,078	_____	33,226	_____
Total	204,625		159,528		132,507	

Source: *Current Population Reports*, P. 20, No. 478, May 1994; *March 1996 Current Population Survey*, Sept. 1996.
[1]Never married, and widowed.
[2]Persons aged 15 and over.

1. Table 13.1 presents data on marital status for all persons 18 years old and over, 15 years old and over for 1996. Calculate the percent distribution for each marital status for every year indicated.

2. How would you describe the changes in the percent divorced for the years presented in the table?

3. The data in Table 13.1 include all persons over the age of 18 years. A more refined method of analyzing divorce patterns is to compare divorced persons to the persons who are married with spouse present as in Table 13.2. Why would this "divorce rate" give a better picture of divorce patterns?

4. Table 13.2 presents divorce rates by race and Hispanic origin.

TABLE 13.2 **Divorced Persons Per 1,000 Married Persons with Spouse Present by Race and Hispanic Origin: 1970–1995**

	1995	1980	1970
White	152	92	44
Black	304	203	83
Hispanic Origin	152	98	61

Source: *Current Population Reports*, P. 20. No. 478; P.20 No. 491, Dec. 1996.

Calculate the percentage increase between 1970 and 1995 for all three groups. The formula for this calculation is:

$$\frac{1995 - 1970}{1970} \times 100 = \begin{array}{l} \text{Percentage Change} \\ \text{1970 to 1995} \end{array}$$

a. White _____

b. Black _____

c. Hispanic origin _____

5. Describe the changes indicated by your calculations.

6. Table 13.3 presents data on living arrangements for children under 18 years old. Based on the data in the table, calculate the percent distribution for both years shown.

TABLE 13.3 Living Arrangements of Children Under 18 Years by Marital Status of Parents: 1992–1995

Living Arrangements	1995		1992	
	Number (1,000)	Percent	Number (1,000)	Percent
Total no. of children	67,214	_____	64,216	_____
Living with both parents	48,276	_____	46,638	_____
Living with mother only	16,477	_____	15,396	_____
Divorced	6,019	_____	5,507	_____
Married, spouse absent	3,901	_____	3,790	_____
Widowed	695	_____	688	_____
Never married	5,862	_____	5,410	_____
Living with father only	2,461	_____	2,182	_____
Divorced	1,181	_____	932	_____
Married, spouse absent	447	_____	491	_____
Widowed	135	_____	165	_____
Never married	696	_____	594	_____

Source: *Current Population Reports*, P. 20, No. 468; P. 20, No. 491, Dec. 1996.

7. For both years shown in Table 3.3, most children are living with _____.

8. What percent of all children were living with their divorced mother in 1992 _____; in 1995 _____?

9. What percent of all children were living with their divorced father in 1992 _____; in 1995 _____?

10. Based on the data in Table 13.3 and your calculations, summarize the major findings on living arrangements of children under the age of 18.

TABLE 13.4   Median Family Income with Children Under Age 18 by Living Arrangements: March 1995

Children Living with Both Parents	$46,195
Living with Divorced Mother	17,789
Living with Divorced Father	28,722

Source: *Current Population Reports*, P. 20, No. 491, Dec. 1996.

11. Another factor important in studying divorce is its economic impact on children. Table 13.4 introduces data on income level and divorce.

a. When compared to households with both parents present, what is the ratio of income for households with divorced mother only? _____

b. Divorced father only? _____

12. What may account for these income differences?

13. How may this impact on the lives of the children?

14. Is divorce as extensive as the mass media has led us to believe?

15. How does the knowledge gained by doing these exercises influence your ideas about getting married?

MODULE **14**

WHY WORRY ABOUT
THE REST OF THE WORLD?

Dissatisfaction with the world in which we live and determina-
tion to realize one that shall be better are the presiding charac-
teristics of the modern spirit.
—GOLDSWORTHY LOWES DICKINSON

In the popular song entitled "We Are the World," the theme of the song is that events that occur anywhere in the world are not isolated occurrences but may have an effect on all of us. In the past, we wouldn't hear about events that occurred in another country, or another state, or even another neighborhood until weeks later, or never at all. Today, with modern communication we learn about events in distant countries as rapidly as do the residents of those countries.

For example, on 7 December 1988, a major earthquake devastated Armenia. Almost instantaneously news of this natural catastrophe spread around the world. Some forty years earlier another quake had struck the Soviet Union. This earlier quake killed 100,000 persons. However, most outsiders and even citizens within the Soviet Union were not aware of this event. Not so, for the more recent event. By 1988, the world had grown too small. Not only do we hear about these events, but very often we are affected by them. The 200 countries on the planet Earth are not isolated units. The connections between different countries are many. Even the so-called superpowers, the United States and Russia, engage in active trade with one another.

There are a number of ways in which we are affected by events in other parts of the world. First, economically, the United States is actively engaged in trade with most of the nations in the world. For example, if you consider your personal belongings, it is highly possible that you have at least one shirt or blouse made in Taiwan, one appliance made in Japan, and perhaps you're driving a new Hyundai from South Korea. Thus our personal consumption patterns are directly connected with many different countries.

Again we may cite the Armenian earthquake as an example of international cooperation. Many Americans and citizens of other countries, upon hearing of the catastrophe, mobilized support for the survivors. Aid, in a variety of forms, was quickly sent into the region. Even the Soviet government, often known for its resistance to outside help, quickly moved to cut the red tape to allow rescue teams into the area. Literally, within days, foreign assistance was on the scene. Such international mobilization of aid would have been unthinkable thirty years ago.

A second example of our connection with the Third World is through both documented and undocumented immigration. Almost daily, newspapers carry stories of immigrants coming across our border from Mexico. There are a number of stories detailing the movement of refugees from Guatemala, El Salvador, and Haiti. There are increasing numbers of Asian immigrants arriving from places such as South Korea and India. One major reason for this pattern of immigration is found in the conditions that exist in the immigrant's native land. Many of these people are fleeing intolerable economic and/or political conditions in their homelands. They may be faced with starvation, unemployment, and political terrorism. If these conditions did not exist, they would not choose to emigrate.

Third, our foreign policy and the manner in which tax dollars are spent is related to events in other countries. Tax dollars that are assigned for foreign aid and the massive outlays of money for defense are two specific ways in which events in other parts of the world affect us. Ultimately, if there is a breakdown in political agreements with other nations, young people such as yourselves may he called upon to serve in the military and go to war to resolve the political disagreements. In addition, there is a moral dimension to this issue. If people are on the verge of starvation, shouldn't we do our best to try to help them? While this module will deal with the more pragmatic elements of this issue, the moral dimension should not be forgotten.

In sum, knowledge about what is occurring in other parts of the world may have great importance to you, affecting your lives directly. As educated adults, college students should become more aware of the international community and of the diversity within this community.

Demographers study population characteristics and trends. They are concerned with population change, birth rates, death rates, fertility rates, and other measures of population. Some demographers are interested in the international community. In looking at all the countries in the world, demographers tend to divide them into two categories: the more developed countries and the less developed countries. The more developed countries would include the two superpowers, the nations of western Europe, and Japan. The less developed countries would include nations in such areas as Sub-Saharan Africa, Latin America, and Asia. While the more developed nations tend to be the stronger nations both economically and militarily, they have smaller populations. Specifically, of the over 5 billion people in the world, only about 20 percent live in the more developed nations. Contrast this with the fact that 37 percent of the world's population—over one-third of the world's population—live in either China or India.

How can we learn more about these other societies? One way we can do this, other than by visiting them, is to examine key demographic data pertaining to these countries. Let us look at some concepts that will illustrate the usefulness of such data. Birth rates and death rates are two key variables used to describe a society. Birth rates tell us how many babies are born in a given year for every 1,000 people in the population. The world, as a whole, had a crude birth rate of 24 in the year 1997. In the same year the crude death rate was 9, which means that for every 1,000 people, there were 9 deaths.

Birth and death rates vary from year to year and from society to society. By comparing these rates one can begin to get a rudimentary picture of a particular society. Societies with large birth and large death rates tend to fall into the less developed category. They tend to have relatively poor health services and traditional attitudes toward birth control and fertility. On the other hand, societies with low birth and death rates tend to fall into the more developed category. They tend to have good health services, and attitudes and practices that promote low fertility.

Two other statistics of interest to demographers are the infant mortality rate and the total fertility rate. The infant mortality rate measures infant deaths. Specifically, it indicates the number of babies born live who die before their first birthday. It is calculated on the basis of every 1,000 births. An infant mortality rate of 59 (the total world rate in 1997) means that for every 1,000 babies born live, 59 died before their first birthday. Many scholars feel this statistic is a very good indicator of a society's well-being. It indicates the quality of its health care. The infant mortality rate is often correlated with a society's level of economic development. The more developed societies have lower infant mortality rates and the less developed societies have higher infant mortality rates.

The total fertility rate (TFR) is a projection. It predicts how many children a woman will have when she has completed her childbearing. There may be a large number of women who are in their childbearing years, fifteen to forty-four years of age. Some of these women have completed having all their children, some plan to have children but have not had any children yet. The TFR predicts what will happen to all these women with respect to the number of children they will eventually have. For example, the current worldwide total fertility rate is 3.0 (1997). This means that for all women between the ages of fifteen and forty-four, when they are finished having all their children, the average number of children will be 3.0 per woman. What this really means is that every 1,000 women will produce 3,000 children. Again, we see substantial differences between the more and less developed countries. The less developed countries have twice the TFR (3.4) than do the more developed countries (1.6).

What are the implications of these differential population trends? Perhaps, the most immediate problem is that of feeding the ever growing number of people on this planet.

If we return to the issues discussed at the beginning of the module, that of economic and political impacts, population patterns have a direct bearing on them. A society with an ever increasing population will have great difficulty achieving economic stability. This is especially true if the country is in the less developed category. Because of population pressures, the society may seek more and more aid from other countries to feed its population and maintain its defensive capabilities. Your tax dollars may be spent helping such societies. If support is not given, the political system in these countries may become unstable, which may create political tensions and may eventually lead to conflict. As noted earlier, this too may have a direct effect on the lives of Americans, especially Americans of college age.

In addition to the problems noted, there are other issues related to population. Illiteracy, environmental pollution, and the quality of life are just a few of the contemporary issues that are affected by population patterns. By having you examine some of these population patterns you will be able to come to a better understanding of the world we live in and some of the major problems that face the planet Earth today.

SOCIAL ISSUES

Why worry about the rest of the world? As noted in the introduction, demographic patterns can give us important clues as to what is occurring in other parts of the world. Let us examine and analyze some of the important patterns.

ANALYSIS

How fast is the world population growing? Examine Table 14.1.

TABLE 14.1 Birth and Death Rates: 1997

	Total Population (Billions)	Crude Birth Rates	Crude Death Rates	Annual % Change	Doubling Time
Worldwide	5,840	24	9	_____	_____
More developed nations	1,175	11	10		
Less developed nations	4,666	27	9	_____	_____
				_____	_____

Source: Adapted from *Population Reference Bureau 1997 World Population Data Sheet.*

1. One important statistic is annual percentage change. This indicates annual increases or decreases in the population. It involves a simple calculation.
   One subtracts the death rate from the birth rate and places a decimal
   point in the middle. For example, if the birth rate is 35 and the death rate
   is 18, the following calculation is made.

$$\text{birth rate} = 35$$

$$\text{death rate} = \frac{18}{17}$$

Annual percent increase = 1.7

Now calculate the annual percent change for the three categories in Table
14.1 and place your results in the appropriate blanks.

2. Demographers often use the concept of doubling time to analyze how
   quickly an area is increasing in population. *Doubling time* is the number of
   years it will take the area to double its present population.

   If a society has a population of 10 million people in 1986, and the doubling time is fourteen years, then, in the year 2000, the population will be
   20 million people. Calculating doubling time is also quite simple. All you
   need to know is the annual percent growth rate. The calculation is based
   upon the rule of 70. You take the annual percentage rate and divide it into
   70; this will give you the number of years it will take for the population to
   double itself.

   We may use the above example of 1.7 percent annual percentage increase to illustrate the calculation.

$$\text{Rule of 70} = \frac{70}{1.7} = 41 \text{ years to double population}$$

Annual percent rate = 1.7

Now calculate the doubling time for the three categories in Table 14.1.

3. Which group of nations has the highest annual percent increase in
   population?

   _____

4. Which group of nations has the fastest doubling time? _____

5. What factors do you believe contribute to the different patterns of growth for developed and developing nations?

6. Why is rapid population growth in developing nations perceived to be a problem?

7. Table 14.2 presents data on infant mortality rates and total fertility rates.

a. If a country has an IMR, of 43 and a TFR, of 4.1, how would you describe this nation?

TABLE 14.2   Infant Mortality and Total Fertility: 1997

	Infant Mortality Rate (IMR)	Total Fertility Rate (TFR)
Worldwide	59	3.0
More developed	9	1.6
Less Developed	64	3.4

Source: Adapted from *Population Reference Bureau 1997 World Population Data Sheet.*

b. If a country has an IMR, of 10 and a TFR, of 1.9, how would you describe this nation?

Let us look next at some specific countries and analyze some of their demographics.

TABLE 14.3 Birth and Death Rates for Selected Countries: 1997

Country	Total Population (millions)	Birth Rate	Death Rate	Annual % Increase	Doubling Times
China	1,236.7	17	7	_____	_____
Italy	57.4	9	9	_____	_____
Japan	126.1	10	7	_____	_____
India	969.7	29	10	_____	_____
Indonesia	204.3	25	8	_____	_____
U.S.	267.7	15	9	_____	_____

Source: Adapted from *Population Reference Bureau 1997 World Population Data Sheet.*

8. Calculate both the annual percent increase and the doubling time for all six countries and place your answers in the appropriate places on the table.

9. Which country is experiencing the fastest growth? _____

10. Which country is experiencing the slowest growth? _____

11. In any one year which country will have the greatest increase in the number of people living in the society? _____

12. Which countries follow the more developed demographic patterns?

_____

13. Which countries follow the less developed demographic patterns?

_____

14. Based upon your data analysis, should you worry about the rest of the world? How might events in the rest of the world affect you personally, and affect society as a whole?